godparents

A Celebration of Those Special People in Our Lives

. . . .

Michelle DeLiso

Contemporary Books

Chicago   New York   San Francisco   Lisbon   London   Madrid   Mexico City
Milan   New Delhi   San Juan   Seoul   Singapore   Sydney   Toronto

The *McGraw-Hill* Companies

Library of Congress Cataloging-in-Publication Data

DeLiso, Michelle.
        Godparents : a celebration of those special people in our lives/
        Michelle DeLiso.
                p.   cm.
        Includes bibliographical references and index.
        ISBN 0-07-139009-X
        1. Sponsors.   I. Title.

        BV1478. D45   2002
        306.87—dc21   2002073677

1 2 3 4 5 6 7 8 9 0   LBM/LBM   1 0 9 8 7 6 5 4 3 2

ISBN 0-07-139009-X

Interior design by Amy Yu Ng

McGraw-Hill books are available at special quantity discounts to use as premiums and sales promotions, or for use in corporate training programs. For more information, please write to the Director of Special Sales, Professional Publishing, McGraw-Hill, Two Penn Plaza, New York, NY 10121-2298. Or contact your local bookstore.

Contents

Preface

This book is the brainchild of my agent, Laura Dail, whose unwavering devotion to the written word always rewards her with great book ideas. After seeing a spate of books about moms, dads, stepparents, aunts, and uncles, Laura thought, "How about a book on godparents?" Godparenting is a topic that is rarely discussed, even though so many of us have close relationships with godparents and godchildren. The timing was uncanny: Laura, a single mother, had just adopted a baby girl and was trying to decide how to approach the selection of godparents. And shortly after I finished the proposal for this book, I found out I was pregnant with my first child. Would my husband and I select godparents after the baby was born? And if so, whom to choose?

I'd never thought much about my own godparents' story until Laura brought up the topic. Their story was unusual at the time that it occurred, although these days it probably doesn't seem so out-of-the-ordinary. I am the product of an interfaith marriage, and during the selection of my godparents back in 1968, my parents faced a challenge. The godparents they wanted to choose for me were nonpracticing Muslim siblings born to a Muslim father, but they had a strong grasp on Catholicism because their mother was Catholic. The church would not allow them to stand as my godparents, though, and my parents had to choose different people.

If our stories were unique, Laura and I thought, there must be hundreds of other godparenting stories waiting to be told. And there were. *Godparents* is dotted with funny, melancholy, informative, inspiring, and unexpected stories from real godparents and godchildren.

While the clergy members I interviewed felt that godparents should stay true to the role's sacred beginnings and cultivate a spiritual relationship with their godchildren, the academic research I reviewed (and the godparents I spoke with) made it clear that the role of godparent has shifted to accommodate individual families within different cultures at different points in history. And the godparents I heard from didn't always think of the role in religious terms. In addition to being spiritual guides, they defined themselves as mentors, protectors, defenders, auxiliary parents, big brothers or sisters, fun-loving coconspirators, and friends. And while it's true that in many cases, the original duties of the role are no longer being performed in practice, the relationships that have flourished as a result of that initial baptismal promise have nourished thousands of children in a myriad of positive ways. There are even "godparents" who have never made baptismal vows, but have gallantly accepted the title and spent a lifetime shepherding their godchildren through all of life's challenges and milestones. Regardless of the way in which the relationship was initiated, godparents can be someone for children to turn to in times of crisis, an adult with whom children can talk when their parents aren't listening, a friend to confide in and innocently conspire with, a mentor from whom to seek educational and vocational guidance, and—in some tragic cases—a support network to tap into when parents could no longer provide.

In Chapter 1 you'll learn about the ancient roots of godparenting and how the custom was used in various cultures to bind families and communities. Chapter 2 will provide you with a general idea of what parents and godparents can expect at a contemporary baptism. Chapter 3 serves up a host of interpretations of godparenting today. Chapter 4 is especially for parents; for now, you are the arbiters of your child's social and spiritual circle. Follow the dictates of your heart and the advice in this chapter, and you just might find the perfect godparents. Chapters 5 and 7 will help current and potential godparents. Read them before you agree to embark on the journey of godparenting. Chapters 6 and 8 let you explore the worlds of fictional and famous godparents, and find advice and gift ideas from everyday godparents whose stories may mirror your own.

Acknowledgments

Many thanks to my agent, Laura Dail, for her creative vision and tireless enthusiasm; my editor, Judith McCarthy, for her patience and gentle guidance; my friend and colleague Lilliam Rivera for always keeping her finger on the pulse of entertainment; Mary Ann Nuzzo at the Federation of Christian Ministries for her thoughtful input, her help with my endless questions, and for being so generous with her time; Marsha Blake at the Theological Seminary's Gardner Sage Library in

New Brunswick, New Jersey; Reverend Monsignor Armando J. Perini at the Church of St. Helena in Edison, New Jersey; Reverend Ellen Little, pastor of the Wesley Foundation, the United Methodist Campus Ministry of Rutgers University in New Brunswick, New Jersey; the Reverends Suzanne and Kevin Hart of Three Bridges Reformed Church in Three Bridges, New Jersey; Jonathan Percival, rector of St. Luke's Episcopal Church in Metuchen, New Jersey; Second Baptist Church in Metuchen, New Jersey; the survey respondents and interviewees for giving so freely of their time and for opening their hearts; my husband for giving me the time and space to finish this book while we were expecting our first baby, Ethan Joseph; my family and friends for their bottomless well of support; and finally, my unofficial godparents—you know who you are.

1

The Birth of Godparents

———●—●—●———

The thing that's cool about godparenting is that it gives someone who is special to your parents a sacred place in your life. [The woman chosen as my godmother] could never be my aunt, but when she became my godmother, we instantly formed a lasting connection. It's a comfort to know that there's someone out there, apart from your immediate family, who is always looking out for you and wishing you well.   —COLLEEN, Roman Catholic

———●—●—●———

Baptism—the start of a lifelong journey of commitment and discipleship—is one of the oldest and most important sacraments in Christianity. Traditionally, it is the ceremony during which godparents are appointed for the child being baptized. Today, baptism is a popular practice celebrated in vastly different ways.

While some view baptism as a ritual and a tradition, others see it as a day to honor their faith, and still others celebrate it as a social event marked by a party. Many families feel it is all of these things. But popular as it may be, the ritual of baptism seems to be one of the least understood sacraments. And godparents often don't know what is expected of them.

If you're about to be part of a baptismal ceremony during which you'll become or name a godparent, what better way to honor the occasion than by taking a look at what baptism meant to early Christians? You'll find out how that meaning has shifted, and learn, too, about the arrival and survival of godparents through the ages. The concept of "godparents" had its beginnings in the earliest times of Christianity, as we'll see. This book will focus on baptism's history and its place in the Christian tradition, but you'll also learn about its many valuable interpretations by other religious and secular traditions.

Early Baptism and Sponsors

In Christian theology, every human being was thought to have two births. The first was a physical birth, which carried one into the physical world. The second was a spiritual birth, or baptism, which delivered a human being from the death of sin into a life of grace where they are one with God. The ritual served as both a spiritual cleansing and an initiation into the church.

Nowadays, the practice of baptism is held most often for infants, but that wasn't always the case. The early Christians—those who inhabited Palestine, Greece, and the Middle East during the first three centuries A.D.—rarely celebrated this ritual for babies. Most of the people baptized during the dawn of Christianity were adults who converted from Greco-Roman polytheism and became followers of the teachings of Jesus.

We know that at least some Christians were baptized during infancy—without debate—during the second century A.D. (Later in history, baptism of children would be debated by some great thinkers, such as Saint Augustine, Saint Hippolytus, and the Roman theologian Tertullian.) It was believed that Adam's sin was present in all of us, including infants, so they would suffer grave consequences if they should die without being baptized. Because of this principle, seriously ill infants underwent the ritual, and it had a special name in these cases: "clinical baptism," from *kline*, the Greek word for "bed." (Clinical baptism later became a traditional procedure in hospitals, often performed by Catholic doctors and nurses.) Infant baptism eventually became the norm, but that happened later in the game.

Christianity was outlawed in the Roman Empire until A.D. 313. Despite that fact, in some areas of the Mediterranean, the burgeoning Christian communities lived in harmony with their non-Christian neighbors. But in other places, Christians were unwelcome in the neighborhood. They lived in fear of being driven out or attacked, and had to keep their worshiping practices under wraps. The Christian neophytes spoke of eating the flesh and drinking the blood of someone else, talked of loving one's brothers and sisters, and didn't believe in the Greco-Roman gods. The flesh-eating and blood-drinking referred to the Body and Blood of Christ, but it sounded fishy to those

In the days of old, baptisms were rarely performed for babies. The ritual was reserved for adults who'd spent three years training for it.

who weren't disciples of Jesus of Nazareth. The early Christians were often suspected of conspiring to commit horrible crimes like cannibalism and incest, and they usually met in secret—a stealthy practice that didn't help their already precarious situation.

Christian society was driven underground for a time because so many congregants lived in fear of religious persecution. Anyone who wanted to inquire about membership in the community would have to do so sotto voce. If the inquirer was thought to be sincere and suitable, he or she was quickly introduced to the congregation. The local assembly would assign one of its members—a sponsor (from the Latin word *spondere*, meaning "to promise")—to make sure the student was worthy of learning the mysteries of salvation. The sponsor was also responsible for providing religious instruction and preparing the student for baptism, the official ceremonial initiation into the church.

The entire church would pray for, and with, the potential disciple because the beginner's conversion was felt to be the community's responsibility. And yet, as close-knit as the community was, the newcomer would sometimes be kept in the dark about certain practices. Because the danger of persecution was palpable, new folks weren't informed of all of the religion's mys-

> **A** sponsor's job included teaching a pupil and protecting the congregation from infiltrators.

teries, nor were they told about the congregation's regular meeting places. A sponsor had to be sure that his or her pupil wouldn't betray the group after gaining entry. In addition to being an instructor, the sponsor had to be a sort of bulwark for the congregation: someone who was always on the lookout for people who wanted to infiltrate the church, intent on reporting the so-called Christian traitors to the authorities.

Testing and Training

As converts proliferated, Christian communities devised elaborate procedures for testing and initiating them. The customs varied by city and century, but all the variations shared common threads. First, a candidate had to be found acceptable—based on both the testimony of those who introduced him or her to the congregation and on the investigation into the candidate's life. The candidate was then admitted as a *catechumen*—a person eligible for the religious training process known as the *catechumenate* (from the Greek word *kathodigisi* meaning "instruction").

This admission was followed by a probationary period, during which the catechumen had to prove his or her sincerity and integrity by displaying ideal behavior. If the candidate's conduct and/or lifestyle was deemed unacceptable, baptism could be delayed—or the aspiring Christian could be permanently expelled from the training he or she was scheduled to begin. Some Christian leaders even had a list of things that might lead to a catechumen's dismissal, such as objectionable sexual practices or demonic possession. Some inquirers would not have been admitted for consideration in the first place—those who made a living doing something immoral such as prostitution or entertaining; something that involved bloodshed, like being a gladiator or a soldier; or a number of other livelihoods considered inappropriate. These inquirers would have had to find a new line of work before they could even have been regarded as serious candidates.

Once a catechumen cleared the probationary hurdle, he or she still had a long journey ahead. These students jumped through hoops in order to be ready for baptism, a ritual that at the time included what would evolve into the sacraments of First Communion and confirmation. To prepare for it, candidates had to be trained, tested, and purified through exorcism. They also had to fast, pray, and undergo "moral formation."

The process, which could last as many as three years, was a structured experience that required the candidates to take a long hard look at their lives. Those elements of preparation became some of the earliest formal structures of the church.

Prebaptism Practices

After successfully completing all the prerequisites, the believer's title would change from *catechumen* to *elect* (from the Latin word *electus*, meaning "one who has been chosen"). *Elect* was the term used in Rome—in other regions where Latin was spoken the elect were called *competentes* (those who seek). In Greece they were *photisomenoi* (those who are to be enlightened).

But even though the students had moved up a rung on the Christian ladder, they were not yet seen as full Christians by those who had already crossed the cardinal threshold of baptism. The candidates were almost ready to undergo this rite, which would signal a pivotal change in their lives. But what did baptism mean to the novices? According to Joseph Martos in his book *Doors to the Sacred*, it "marked a dividing line between the old and the new, between waiting for the messiah and finding him, between living with guilt and living with forgiveness, between being in a community of law and being in a community of love."

The candidates had been told that as catechumens they could consider themselves "Christians," but that after being baptized they would be ushered into a community that referred to its members as "the faithful." Several weeks prior to the baptismal ceremony, which was held only once a year, those pupils chosen to be fully initiated would embark on a more intense period of groundwork. The candidates were presented to the bishop and their sponsors attested to their worthiness. They were exorcised of evil spirits each Sunday and were continually blessed and anointed as the induction reached a crescendo. In the final week of the initiation they were instructed each day and had their lives reinspected. At this time, candidates would learn the Lord's Prayer and the Apostle's Creed. They fasted for two days before the ceremony.

The Old Baptismal Rite

On the eve of Easter, proceedings began in front of the bishop and the congregation. The paschal candle was lit—symbolizing Christ, the light of the world—and it illuminated the dark place where they prayed. The candidates listened to hymns and Bible readings all through the night. At dawn, they followed the bishop and his assistants to the baptismal pool. After a blessing of the water, the soon-to-be faithful were anointed and exorcised one last time. Disrobed, the men (chaperoned by the deacons) and the women (accompanied by the deaconesses) were led into the pool to be partially immersed. In some ceremonies, those being baptized would first face the west where the sun sets into darkness, to renounce Satan, and then would turn to the east toward the light of dawn, to accept Christ. Water was poured over them in intervals as they responded to questions attesting to their faith. They were asked if they believed in God, in his son Jesus, in the Holy Spirit, and in the Church. The reply to these questions was, of course, "I do believe." Water was poured over them after each reply. After exiting the pool, they were once again anointed and presented with a white garment, which they would wear and keep clean for the duration of Easter. As they presented themselves to the bishop, they were anointed yet again. Officially baptized, they became members of the church.

After the completion of this dramatic, somber ceremony, a sponsor's job was done. His or her contractual agreement was fulfilled, and this character witness-cum-teacher had no additional obligations in the life of the new believer.

In ancient times, the venue for the baptism was almost as spectacular as the event itself. Special buildings called *baptisteries* were erected for baptisms. They were always situated close to (or connected with) a church. The baptistery's roughly circular architectural form evoked the shape of Roman buildings that had been designated for religious purposes. But baptisteries were usually octagonal, an optical metaphor for the number eight, which symbolized a new beginning in Christian numerology. They were usually roofed with a dome, symbolizing the heavenly realm toward which the believer progresses after baptism. Many baptisteries were large and elaborately decorated, such as the ones found in Florence, Italy; in Parma, Italy; and in Poitiers, France.

After the sixth century, baptisteries were gradually reduced to small chapels within churches. By the tenth century, when affusion (pouring of water over the head) became

Centuries ago, baptisms took place in baptisteries—special buildings constructed just for that ceremony.

customary, baptisteries weren't used at all. And in modern churches, the font alone serves for baptism. But the remnants of early symbolism have withstood the passage of time; the font's usual location near the church door suggests that it serves as a portal into Christian life.

Baptism of Babies

Between the fourth and sixth centuries A.D., an enormous change took place. The Roman world, from Britain to Egypt, became Christian by law; the religion was protected and preferred by the later Roman emperors. Christianity—which became the official religion of the empire around A.D. 380—was incorporated as a central feature of Roman culture. It was no longer necessary to worship underground. Baptism was seen not only as a rite of entry into the church, it also granted a person citizenship of the state.

No longer banned from all the mysteries of Christianity, catechumens were finally permitted to attend public worship services almost in their entirety (Holy Communion still remained a mystery to them until later in their training), and the restrictions on acceptable occupations began to loosen up. But as the years wore on, there weren't too many catechumens left to attend mass because the number of adult converts was dwindling. Christian families of the empire were having babies, and those infants logically became the ordinary candidates for baptism. And remember, the belief that babies who died without a baptism had no chance for salvation was still prevalent. The child's soul would rest in a questionable state—some were believed to be in purgatory and others would go to hell. This idea, together with the fact that infant mortality was so common in those days, compelled parents to baptize newborns even before the standard yearly liturgical baptism was offered. Because infants couldn't be instructed, the catechumenate all but vanished, and the ritual of baptism changed to accommodate the typical candidate's age.

One of the changes to the ritual involved the water rite. The water ritual for infants often involved complete immersion because it was easier than the partial immersion and pouring of the water that was done for adults. But the ritual varied by region. Babies might be immersed a single time, three times, or not immersed at all (in which case the water would be poured over their heads). And the lengthy baptismal ritual was abbreviated, too. While adults had been completing an initiation replete with the practices we now know as First Communion and confirmation, infants could undergo only the water ritual. And because the Christian community was so large and geographically diffuse, it was impossible to have the single ritual combining baptism, confirmation, and the Eucharist at the traditional Easter vigil. In order to do that, the bishop would have had to greet all the newly baptized and confirm their baptisms. Villagers could not always make the trek to the central church, nor could the bishop get to all the scattered villages in one year. The bishop continued to baptize some adults, but he more often baptized babies.

The Arrival of Godparents

Another obvious difference between adult and infant baptisms was that in adult baptisms, the converts were able to speak for themselves and state their beliefs; babies, naturally, could not. Because the little ones were unable to respond appropriately during their own initiation, it was chiefly the natural parents' job to speak and act on the infant's behalf, and to present the infant on baptism day. Adults were asked if they believed in Christ, everlasting life, and in certain creeds. The same questions were asked at infant baptisms, but the parents would answer on behalf of the baby and promise to raise the child in the faith. In some areas of the Christian world, outside sponsors were invited to the baptism to stand in place of the natural parents, a practice which gained popularity along with the notion that each child had two births—one physical, the other spiritual.

Having a witness stand at infant baptisms was a practice that may have been borrowed from a Judaic custom. At a ritual Jewish circumcision—called *bris* (from the Hebrew *bêrith*, meaning "covenant")—a witness (always a Jew, but not necessarily a relative) holds the baby while the procedure is performed. The man holding the baby is called the *sandek*, and is in the most honored position a bris participant can hold. The word *sandek* is commonly translated as "godfather"; it could possibly be derived from the Greek word *syntekos*, meaning "companion of child."

In the Middle Ages, two additional individuals were honored by being included at the bris: the *kvater* and the *kvaterin*. Often a married couple or a brother and sister, the *kvater* and *kvaterin* would assist the sandek. They were sometimes considered the boy's godmother and godfather. The words *kvater* and *kvaterin* are most likely Polish-Yiddish corruptions of the German word for godfather: *gevatter*.

By the eighth century, both Latin and Byzantine Christianity forbade parents to sponsor their own children. The physical and spiritual births were believed to be so essentially different that they needed to be distinguished as such, by having two sets of parents to represent a baby during the baptismal ritual. The sponsors were the parents in the child's second, or spiritual, birth. The church accepted and encouraged this form of "parenthood in God," and took steps to shape its religious role. Buoyed by the church, the sponsors—whom we can now refer to as godparents—helped the baby to be baptized in a liturgy that was originally composed for adults.

During the lengthy service, each child had to be carried, undressed and dressed, and offered to the clergy at certain moments. The act of taking the baby, dripping wet, immediately after the water rite came to be viewed as the crucial moment in creating a godparental relationship. Lifting the baby from the waters of the baptismal font has been described as a gesture reminiscent of a midwife lifting a newborn from his or her mother's womb. It was even common in some cultures to ask midwives to be godmothers of the babies they helped bring into the world.

The Role of Godparent

Godparents were spiritually important in a child's life, but the relationship also carried social significance; it united a non–family member with the child and his or her parents, thereby creating obligations. The godparents were expected to take a special interest in the child's spiritual and material welfare. The bond was reinforced much as it is today, by gift-giving, visiting, investing time, and showing affection. Children, in turn, were expected to respect their godparents. Although the godparental relationship developed secular implications, most participants clearly viewed the relationship as a sacred, pure, and holy one. Its unique nature was confirmed by a ban on marriage and romantic relationships between godparent and godchild.

The early sponsors mentioned at the beginning of this chapter have often been referred to as the first godparents. But it's clear that a sponsor's role was vastly different from a godparent's role. Early sponsors had the specific task of preparing an adult for baptism, making sure his or her life was exemplary *before* initiating the candidate into the baptismal ritual. Moreover, marital taboos did not apply to the sponsors—they could enter into a romantic relationship with the baptizee. Godparents were considered the "spiritual parents" in the second birth of the child, whereas sponsors fulfilled a nonparental, short-term contract. Sponsors had no obligations to the parents of the new believer, and the relationship with that convert lasted only as long as the training period. In some cases, the relationship between a particular sponsor and student ended before the training period came to a close because it was common to have more than one sponsor preside over the three-year schooling period (one for the instruction period, a second for baptism, and a third for confirmation). Godparents, on the other hand, promise a lifelong commitment to help instruct a child in the faith, beginning with that child's baptism. They make that promise to both the child and his or her parents, implying a lifelong relationship among all of them.

Godparenting Around the Globe

Over time, and throughout the world, the godparent/godchild relationship has shifted as the relationship's practitioners have molded its tenets to suit the demands of their respective societies. Renaissance-era Florence is a good example of how the selection of godparents reached beyond the promise of spiritual upbringing and took on remarkable social and political implications. Research suggests that Florentine parents would choose anywhere from three to thirty godparents for their child. The Florentine church eventually ruled that three godparents per child would suffice.

It was thought sensible to put a cap on the number of "baptismal kin" one could acquire. The reason? If you had too many, it was easy to forget your own godparents, and even easier to forget your godparents' children. If spiritual links were forgotten, a person might unwittingly marry a baptismal relative and by doing so, commit spiritual incest. If a child had thirty godparents, imagine how many baptismal kin he or she would inherit—the Florentines could have made a full-time career out of keeping track! But many Florentines paid the "three only" rule no mind and went on to choose a number of friends and neighbors to play the part. (They rarely asked male relatives to be godfathers, but they did look to the family for godmothers.) Some parents even had the entire town serve as "godparent" to the child.

These godparents were connected not only to their godchildren, but also to the parents who elected them, making them "co-parents." Electing co-parents seems to have helped biological parents gain and reward friends. The choice of godparents was heavily influenced by the idea that certain people could help alleviate political unrest, aid in foreign policy, or protect one from hostile tax assessments. But that didn't necessarily mean that parents picked co-parents of a higher social status. Some were chosen as "acts of charity." The archaic, private ledgers of Florentine men—the *ricordanze*—revealed that some godparents were chosen "for the love of God" (*per amor di dio*). The phrase meant that those selected were not obligated to give gifts to the godchildren; rather, the natural parents were expected to extend gifts to those they had chosen. Those nominated "for the love of God" were often paupers, disabled, or religious officials.

Godparent selection in Renaissance-era Florence had the potential to be socially catastrophic. Often, men of high social or political standing would approach fathers and *request* to stand as godfather to a child. Imagine the predicament a father would find himself in if he declined the offer! For example, it was said that the former king of France, Louis XI, wanted to be godfather to Lucrezia de'Medici, daughter of the Florentine statesman and ruler Lorenzo de'Medici. But Lorenzo had someone else in mind for godfather: Galeazzo Sforza, the Duke of Milan. The duke was bumped to placate the king, but fortunately, Sforza didn't seem to take offense—in fact, he later asked Lorenzo to be godfather to *his* child, an act that is believed to have reaffirmed their friendship.

Godparenting also had important practical functions in village and rural life. In the countryside, landlords would sometimes ask their sharecroppers to be co-parents. It wasn't because parents wanted the share-croppers to have a spiritual relationship with their children; it was more a means of ironing out wrinkles in tense relationships. These baptismal kinship coalitions helped to alleviate the pressures that resulted from an oppressive economic arrangement. It was much like the early Latin American institution of *compadrazgo* (an institution brought over by the Europeans, which we'll visit later in this chapter).

The male-centered Florentine culture offers us a skewed view of godparenthood through the *ricordanze*. The men mainly recorded information for and about themselves and their male offspring, with only an occasional nod to godmothers. Nevertheless, it is known that godmothers played a significant role. Church law required that godmothers attend baptisms, and they often had to appear in lieu of the biological mother, who was usually still recovering from childbirth. Even those new mothers who were able to participate may have chosen not to because of a taboo that forbade a woman to enter sacred space for forty days after the birth of a baby, a time during which a woman was considered religiously unclean.

It was a common practice for women to choose godmothers for their children, while men chose the godfathers. The criteria were different for each god-parent. Friends, midwives, wet nurses, and relatives were common choices for godmothers, as was anyone else who had helped with the baby's physical birth.

In Sweden, baptism and godparenting acquired their own flavor. In some areas, a child could have as many as twelve godparents. And according to Swedish church law of the late seventeenth century, baptism had to take place within eight days of a birth (another concept perhaps borrowed from Judaism, since the bris, the Jewish ritual circumcision, traditionally took place eight days after a baby boy's birth). Lutherans with knowledge of the catechism were the only people permitted to witness the baptism. Like Italy, Sweden's doctrines did not require the mother's presence at the ceremony, and economic status was a determining factor for the selection of godparents. Some shopkeepers would invite witnesses from social classes above their own to their children's baptism, especially when the baby was a boy. A boy would ultimately inherit the family business, and it would have been in his best interest to have ties to

New mothers sel-dom went to their baby's baptism. God-mothers would proudly stand in for them.

influential and well-to-do community members. Those members were likely to be able to provide assistance in times of financial crisis.

In eighteenth- and nineteenth-century France, god-parenting took a different twist. In certain regions of the country, very specific cul-tural rules existed to govern the choice of godparents. Par-ents had to name godparents from the family pool, begin-ning with grandparents and followed by uncles, aunts, brothers, and sisters. It wasn't much of a selection process at all—it was obvious whom they were *required* to ask. And it was only after those specific rela-tives were exhausted that par-ents could venture outside the family circle. It was also customary that an equal number of relatives be chosen from each side of the family; a child's baptism served to confirm the union of two families that had been joined by marriage.

Young Swedish boys destined to inherit the family store would likely have wealthy godparents who could help out when business wasn't booming.

France had another unique requirement—parents often had no say in what to name their own children. It was the godparent that named his or her own godchild, quite often naming the baby after himself or herself. The baby would receive his or her name at the font, making the name a religious marker admitting one into the Christian community. This was a godparental practice that was not mandated by the church, but the church didn't challenge it.

When the Spaniards arrived in the New World, they introduced a European custom that went hand-in-hand with godparenting, a practice that came to be known as *compadrazgo*. Compadrazgo is the unique relationship that develops between a godparent and the adult (usually the parent) who appointed him or her. The longtime inhabitants of the New World and the newly arrived Spaniards used compadrazgo in a number of secular ways.

Colonial-era Lima, Peru, provides an example of how this relationship worked. Limenos adopted the custom in hopes of stabilizing family life and providing mutual support in the face of epidemic-related deaths. The elite Spanish families used the institution as a means of bonding with subordinate Spaniards and Peruvians, in order to maintain social control over them. Through this relationship, the colonizing landowners gained the trust of the local leaders, and were able to arrange for laborers on an informal basis rather than relying on the formal labor resources.

The *curacas*—the Peruvian community leaders—developed these godparent-related ties with the Spaniards because they saw the connection as a means of access to financial resources, business skills, and contacts. Having a Spanish godparent to manage one's estate would be a definite benefit. In turn, the link to the curacas could help the Spaniards rent or buy the leaders' property, as well as that of the leaders' relatives.

Ultimately, implementing this form of godparenting seems to have backfired on the community leaders because it weakened communities: the leaders compromised their authority and traditions, and made it easier for outsiders to move into and take their land.

While Christians abroad were implementing and modifying godparenting, early North America had its own variations. Pittsburgh, Pennsylvania, saw an influx of Hungarians in the late 1800s and early 1900s. The immigrants who settled there—originally from all areas of Hungary—developed their own criteria for godparent selection. Typically, the parents chose godparents who came from the same Hungarian village or county as they did, and it was not uncommon to have the same godparents serve more than one sibling. They maintained regional ties even when that meant crossing religious lines. Lutherans sometimes chose Roman Catholic godparents, and one baptismal entry for a child found a Greek Catholic godfather and a Calvinist god-mother. Godparents were seen as the spiritual parents and guardians of their godchildren, and parents thought seriously about who could best serve. In turn, godparents considered their election to be an honor.

We'll see in later chapters that religion, local customs, and individual preferences have sired a host of interpretations of this role. It seems that no other "familial" title has reconstructed its anatomy as many times, and in as many ways, as that of godparent.

2

What Happens at a Baptism or a Naming Ceremony?

* * *

Our daughter's godparents are the people in our lives to whom we feel the closest—my sister-in-law (my best friend) and a childhood friend of my husband's. When we named these godparents, we had a traditional baptism in the church where three generations of my family had been baptized. My daughter wore a christening gown that was over sixty years old and had been worn by her father, her godmother, many cousins,

aunts, et cetera. After the baptism, we had a celebration. Tradition should play a very large part in
this event—it brings everyone together and
creates a true family bond.   —MONIQUE, Methodist

———————●—●—●———————

Baptism—a term that traces its roots to the Greek
word *bapto*, meaning "to dip" or "to immerse"—has
a colorful history. The sacrament has been adapted to
meet the needs of both adults and infants. Once a
cleanser of original sin, baptism's purpose shifted to sig-
nify a person's entrance into Christian life. According
to the Gospels, the prophet John the Baptist baptized
Jesus in the river Jordan, and Christians have baptized
the followers of Jesus ever since. It is the rite that wel-
comes a child into faith and fellowship. It is the rite that
empowers one to complete the sacraments of First
Communion and confirmation. It is the commencement of a lifelong process.

Ironically, baptism is simultaneously one of the
most personal and one of the most public events in a
person's spiritual life. For many families, the event
draws an entourage. It can be easy to find more than

forty people in one's family and social group who will turn out for the occasion. In July 2001, Canadian pop vocalist Celine Dion and her husband, Rene Angelil, had their son, Rene Charles, baptized at Quebec's Notre-Dame Basilica. It was reported that 250 family members and guests were in attendance, and the ceremony was also broadcast live throughout Canada.

The number of guests will automatically increase if the baptism takes place during a regular church service. Some families choose to keep the event relatively private, with only the parents, godparents, and immediate family in attendance. On New Year's Day 2002, musician Eric Clapton had both of his daughters baptized in this type of private ceremony. Six-month-old Julia Rose, whom Clapton fathered with his then-girlfriend Melia McEnery, and sixteen-year-old Ruth, his

Presbyterians baptize at any age, but they do not appoint godparents. On occasion, a witness will stand at a baptism.

daughter from a former relationship with Yvonne Kelly, were baptized in St. Mary Magdalen Church just southwest of London. Moments after the ritual, Clapton motioned to the vicar and pleasantly surprised the small crowd of about twenty by marrying Julia Rose's mommy.

But even those couples who try to keep the event low-key can be unsuccessful—especially if one of the partners is one of the most photographed women in the world. Madonna and her film-director husband, Guy Ritchie, attempted to keep the December 2000 baptism of their four-month-old son, Rocco, a relatively private affair. But when family and guests arrived at Scotland's Dornoch Castle, it was surrounded by hundreds of fans, some of whom even climbed trees in hopes of catching a glimpse of the celebrities. And two men were later arrested for trying to record the ceremony in the cathedral.

It is clear that this event can be a private or very public gathering depending on a family's customs, preference, and particular circumstances. But what exactly happens during the ceremony?

The Contemporary Baptism

The ritual has dozens of varying components. It almost always employs water and the Trinitarian invocation, "I baptize you in the name of the Father, and of the Son, and of the Holy Spirit." But there are countless local differences. There are more than twenty-two thousand separate churches, sects, and denominations around the globe that make up the Christian faith today. It would be unrealistic to try to incorporate all of the local varieties here, so let this chapter serve as a general guide.

If you are a parent having your child baptized, you should check with your church ahead of time and ask that the procedures of the ceremony be explained to you so you'll know what to expect. (Some churches even offer educational programs that will familiarize participants with the ceremony, the meaning of its components, the symbolism of the acts and instruments used, and what each participant's role will entail. If that is not an option, ask your church liaison to provide a copy of the ceremony's itinerary so you can review it.) But rest assured, baptism presiders will be there to guide parents and godparents through the ritual on baptism day.

In many communities, the parents and the baby are the key players in the ceremony. The parents hold and

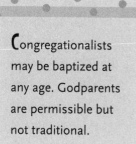

Congregationalists may be baptized at any age. Godparents are permissible but not traditional.

present the baby at different points during the ritual. Godparents, when they are included in a ceremony, are significant, but today they are not as vital as the parents—the child's primary instructional unit—even though years ago the mother herself seldom attended the baptism of her own child. Because babies used to be baptized within days of the birth, mothers were usually still in recovery or preparing for the repast that followed the ceremony. Therefore, godmothers would stand in for them. And if parents were in attendance, they ordinarily held an auxiliary role. That has shifted with time as the nuclear family (rather than the town or village) has become the child's primary community, the community that will set an example of practicing faith and values on a daily basis.

Episcopalians and Lutherans require godparents or sponsors for their children.

When one of the parents is in charge of holding the infant, the officiant or presider will incorporate the godparents in other ways. A godparent might mark the baby with the sign of the cross, read from the Bible, or hold and light the paschal candle (also called the Easter or Resurrection candle). However, some officiants prefer that one of the godparents, usually the god-mother, hold the child during the ceremony and dramatically present the baby to the parents after the water ritual. This practice stems from the belief that baptism is the spiritual birth of the infant, the time when godparents officially mark the beginning of their promise. Some of the early

Attention parents! Don't be shy about your dreams for your child. Write a special prayer for your son or daughter and present it at the baptism or naming ceremony.

baptismal fonts even had the shape of a womb, emphasizing this new and spiritual birth.

Some parents write a personalized prayer or a wish list for the baby that includes their dreams for that child. If this is something you would like to contribute to the ceremony, consult with the baptism coordinator ahead of time to find out if a few moments can be reserved for you to present it. If time does not allow, you can always share it at a gathering after the ceremony.

The baptismal ceremony typically has four parts: the child's introduction, the observation of God's word (which incorporates prayers and readings from the Bible), the water ritual, and the conclusion. Here is a general idea of what you can expect to see within each of those sections.

The Child's Introduction

The ceremony will begin with the officiant welcoming all the guests in attendance. He or she will stress the importance of this gathering as a sign of the faithful community into which the child is being baptized. Some presiders may invite friends and relatives with cameras and camcorders to come forward so that they can be seated near the font, where they'll be able to record everyone in the ceremony. The presider will ask the parents for the name of the baby, and will ask the parents if they wish that the baby (referred to by name) receive the sacrament of baptism. The parents say yes, and the presider reminds them that they are responsible for raising the child in the faith. The presider usually reminds everyone why baptism is performed, and may explain that he or she is following the command of Jesus in the Gospel according to Matthew to "baptize all nations in the name of the Father and of the Son and of the Holy Spirit" (Matthew 28: 18–20). The presider will ask if the parents and godparents understand the commitment they are promising to begin on that day. The child is then welcomed into the community—this is signified, in some denominations, by marking the child's forehead with the sign of the cross, first by the presider, then by the parents and godparents.

Methodists baptize at any age and the baptizee has at least one sponsor.

This part of the ceremony may be a little different from how it's been described here if the baptism is held as part of a mass or service. Some churches offer one or more services a month where babies are baptized. For pragmatic reasons, when held during a larger service, the baptism might be at the beginning of the service because babies can get fussy. Or quite often there will be a day set aside when ten or twelve babies are baptized outside of regular services.

Observation of God's Word

Prayers and readings—usually pertaining to baptism or water—are offered. The presider, parents, godparents, or another family member may read them. All will be invited to pray together for the baby, the parents, and for all those present that they may be good examples for this baby. The presider then offers a healing prayer and anoints the baby's chest with oil. (Sometimes this part is omitted, depending on your church.) The oil is known as the "oil of salvation" (also called the "oil of baptism" or "oil of the catechumens"). It's used in the baptismal ritual as a reminder that blessed oil has been a tool of strength and healing since the early days of Christianity. Oil had, and still has, many important uses in daily life, such as cooking, cleaning, healing, and as a facilitator of light and heat. When this rite is included, it is often done in the early part of the baptismal ritual as a sign of healing.

The Water Ritual

Water is blessed before its use in the baptism. (In some churches, it is blessed only once a year by the bishop and the priest of the diocese.) The baptismal water recalls the purification bath of the early Christians. Symbolically, it represents several things, including new life, new birth, physical and spiritual cleansing, and growth.

Water is a major part of the initiation process, just as the "chaotic waters" are a significant part of the creation story in the first verses of Genesis. The element of water has been dominant across many cultures and religions: ritual immersion plays an important part in Judaism as a symbol of purification and consecration; the ancient Romans had hundreds of baths lining their cities; the ancient Greeks employed water to wash away guilt; and Hindus bathe in the Ganges. One Methodist minister tells the story of how, one year, she brought back holy water from the river Jordan and added drops of it to the baptismal water in the font at the baptisms she presided over, as a special touch to the ceremony.

Depending on family custom, the infant may be dressed in a christening gown for the water ritual. Many families bring the infant to the church already dressed in the gown. (Some families have gowns that are specially made, or are heirlooms passed from one generation to the next.) If a child is to be baptized by immersion, the parents are advised to have the baby wear casual clothes. After the water immersion, the parents and godparents dress the baby in the white gown.

Godparents are not part of the United Church of Canada's tradition, but parents can choose them if they want to.

Sometimes the baby is clothed in a diaper and wrapped in a blanket, which would be taken off (along with the diaper, if the parents think it's safe!) so he or she can be immersed. The infant is then baptized with the holy water.

Depending on the church, the presider will be either a "passive celebrant" or an "active celebrant." The passive celebrant uses the Trinitarian invocation in the passive voice: "[Baby's name] is baptized in the name of the Father, and of the Son, and of the Holy Spirit," thus placing more focus on the active love of God and less on the celebrant. Where the presider is an active celebrant working to follow the command of Jesus to "baptize all nations," the Trinitarian invocation is declared in the active voice: "[Baby's name], I baptize you in the name of the Father, and of the Son, and of the Holy Spirit."

In the Eastern Orthodox tradition, the child is immersed three times in the baptismal font.

Then, the child will either be immersed (where a presider lowers the naked child into the water feet first up to his or her shoulders) in the baptismal font, or will have water poured or sprinkled over his or her forehead. Many feel that this kind of total immersion truly gives the sense of new life and new beginnings. But when it comes to actual initiation into the church, it doesn't matter how much water is used, or how the child is blessed with that water; the baptism is still valid.

At this point in the ceremony, a minister or family member may read more scripture relating specifically to water. Some ministers may have all those closest to the font put a hand somewhere on the baby's body, so that through the act of touch they can personally bless and welcome the baby into the church community. It is the custom in some churches to have each godparent hold the baby and walk in a circle around the font.

A godparent's relationship with his or her godchild officially starts when the baby is lifted from the font. But many godparents will tell you that the relationship can begin way before that moment.

A candle is lit from the church's paschal candle and is presented to a member of the family, usually to one of the godparents. Some families decorate the baptismal candle with paint or nail polish, incorporating the baby's initials or baptismal symbols such as water or the cross. Baby-specific merchants even sell personalized baptismal candles. The candle may be lit by the baby's father, after which the father and godfather hold the candle together. Or, alternately, the godfather alone lights and holds the candle. The officiant reminds them that it is the light of Christ, and should be burned briefly each year on the anniversary of the baby's baptism.

The Conclusion

In some churches, the officiant applies chrism (the same perfumed, blessed oil that is used in confirmation and in the ordination of bishops, priests, and deacons) to the top of the baby's head. This symbolizes service to the people of God. The oil is meant to strengthen those baptized as they begin their lifelong journey.

If the child has not already been wearing a white baptismal garment throughout the ceremony, he or she may be given one at this point. (Some churches use a small white garment that they purchase specifically for the baptisms of their congregants. Other churches have baptismal teams that coordinate everything from the education of the parents to the production of handmade white garments.) It may have the emblem of the cross or a symbol of water embroidered on it. The garment is a sign of the child's Christian dignity and the new era upon which he or she has embarked.

The presider may then invite all present to thank God for the gift that has been given on this day—the child's entrance into a spiritual relationship with his or her Creator. The presider or the parents may raise the child up in the air to be dramatically presented to the congregation, a gesture met with applause. If time has been set aside, a family member might present a short prayer that he or she has written for that child.

The ceremony concludes with the Lord's Prayer. There may be music, but it is usually low-key. Perhaps an organist or a cantor will perform. Some presiders will walk up and down the center aisle with the baby as a way to welcome him or her into the church.

The parents are usually given the baptismal candle to be placed in safekeeping until it is burned again for other ceremonies, including the anniversary of the baby's baptism, his or her First Communion, and confirmation. Still later, the candle may be given to the child to keep when he or she enters into a vocation or married life. The baptismal garment is often given to the parents as a remembrance of that day, along with a baptismal certificate (sometimes called a baptismal remembrance). The certificate will indicate the name and birth date of the child, the names of the child's parents and sponsors or godparents, the date of baptism, and the names of the church and the officiant. A copy is kept in the church's local registry. Godparents may also each be given a certificate, or a specially printed card reminding them that they have accepted the role of sacramental sponsorship and that they are to be models for the candidate.

Naming Ceremonies

There is a growing movement in various places around the world to provide families with a nonreligious alternative to baptism. This effort has been spurred by the increasing number of parents who are searching for a way to welcome new babies into the family and into the world, but are uncomfortable with the idea of making religious promises. They may be among the growing number of couples who are opting for civil marriage ceremonies instead of formal church weddings. The movement is also a response to clergy who are disinclined to perform christenings for infants whose parents don't otherwise attend church, and to family-policy enthusiasts interested in raising awareness—in venues outside the church—about the importance of parenting in strengthening family life.

Enter the baby-naming ceremony. There is, of course, no formal set of purposes and procedures for a naming celebration, since it may be held for any number of reasons: to officially welcome a baby into the family and community; to formally mark names given to children; to welcome adopted children, regardless of age, into the family and community; to provide a way for parents to publicly declare their love and support for their children; and to elect and formally recognize adults who have agreed to play a special and significant adult role in the child's life. These adults are the secular equivalent of godparents.

It's possible that this kind of naming ceremony is the secular cousin of the baby-naming ritual for Jewish girls. When a Jewish girl is born, she formally receives her Hebrew name when her father goes to synagogue, usually at the first Sabbath service that follows her birth. The father is called to the Torah and special prayers are offered for the new baby and her mother. The Hebrew name that the parents have chosen is officially announced.

Like baptisms, naming ceremonies can be elaborate and crowded or pared down and private. Because naming ceremonies are not subject to canonical law, they can be custom-made to suit the parents' needs, wishes, and vision. The ceremony can be held in the venue of the family's choice, such as a backyard or a party hall, and can incorporate any number of celebratory practices: dining and dance, poetry readings, presentation of wish lists, toasts, speeches, unique symbolism, and so on. There is even an organization in England, the Baby Naming Society, that helps parents and families arrange naming ceremonies by offering options and connecting them with local authorities that may know individuals willing to officiate.

Parents can appoint as many or as few sponsors for the child as they choose, and can ask these individuals to make a public affirmation of their pledge to guide/protect/support/mentor the child throughout his or her life. It's a public acceptance of an enormous commitment, an affirmation that may reassure parents of its sincerity when declared in a public setting.

3

The Role of Godparents Today

I've never been asked to be a godparent, though lots of my friends and colleagues have. It seems to be an important role, a role I would take seriously if given the opportunity. I don't think it's about God or religion, though it must still be for a lot of folks. It seems to me the role is more about mentoring and guiding children, and seeing to their emotional development. It's about offering adult friendship to a child. If I were a parent, I think I'd choose godparents based on their ethics; ethics that are similar to mine regardless of their religious upbringing.

—**HELENE, no religion specified**

Language is fluid and dynamic, and so, it seems, are the roles we house under the broad umbrella of the word *family*. How many times have you heard someone refer to a person in his or her life as *sister, brother, mother, cousin, uncle,* or *auntie,* when you know that, technically, they didn't acquire the title by blood or marriage? We often use these familial appellations to refer to those significant individuals in our lives whose loyalty, support, and presence deserve a name that honors the part they've played. They may have supported you through your darkest hours; they've championed you when others assumed you'd fail; they've congratulated you on your accomplishments or called just to say hello when it seemed the rest of the world was too busy. Sometimes the term "dear friend" just doesn't do them justice. They've become family.

This can also be true in the case of godparents. We've uncovered the role's linguistic and conceptual heritage in Chapter 1. It's understood that traditionally, godparents are to see to the Christian upbringing of the godchildren in their charge, especially in the event that the parents can no longer fulfill that responsibility. But over time, we've come to use the term *godparent* in both its traditional form and what I'll call its contemporary form. The contemporary form is agile. It often refers to whomever we choose to bestow the name upon, even if that person hasn't taken spiritual vows at a baptism.

Some will argue that *godparent* doesn't apply in the contemporary sense. After all, the term's origins are spiritual, religious even, and the role was designed to help raise a child in the faith. Therefore, one might as well separate the word "god" from "parent" and perhaps call these people "guideparents" instead. And others may believe that any longstanding parent-like relationship that benefits the life of a child can be considered "godparental."

But one might also say that as society changes and evolves, so do the terms we use to describe our amended roles within that society. Christianity, the faith that has long celebrated godparents, has become the largest of the world's religions. Geographically, it is the most widespread, with a following of some two billion believers. And the role has had some twenty centuries to evolve within multiple cultures around the globe. Is it any wonder that the passage of time and the perseverance of local differences have created the diverse vista of godparenting we see today?

Additionally, many people today choose to define themselves as "spiritual," rather than as followers of any one organized religion. Those individuals whose spirituality is self-defined have unique interpretations of a godparent's role, too, expanding the vista's horizon with each new interpretation.

Unofficial and Honorary Godparents

It is not uncommon for families to bring the practice of godparenting with them when they convert to another denomination, even if the new denomination does not recognize godparenting in the same way those families define it. For example, the Reformed and Methodist Churches have sponsors, but godparenting, as we have defined it previously, is not included in their traditions. However, in the Reformed Church tradition, parenting is seen as a responsibility that's shared between a child's parents and the congregation. Like godparents, the church members make a collective promise to nurture the spiritual development of the baptized child. And some of the clergy members I spoke with told me that it is not out of the ordinary for Methodists or Reformed Church congregants to ask if they can have godparents honored in the baptismal service for their children. It's possible that this happens in other denominations, too.

Clearly, those congregants have taken a practice from another religious tradition and are making an effort to continue that practice in their new faith. The result over time is that the language moves over, making its way with good intentions into denominations that historically have not woven the role into their philosophies. Godparenting has even made its way, unofficially, into Judaism. Jews are not required to select godparents, but many admire the custom and have adopted it.

Some respondents to my own informal godparenting survey called themselves godparents, or had godparents, even though those individuals hadn't taken vows in a church. One story was particularly compelling. Matt, an attorney in Washington, D.C., has two people in his life that he refers to as his godparents, even though they never took baptismal vows. Before Matt was born, his mother, Posy, and future godmother, Sharon, met on an airplane bound for Cuba. The women became fast friends. Sharon even flew to Atlanta with her partner, Jim, to visit Posy after she had given birth to Matt. They were among the first people to visit and hold Matt after he was born, and it was then that Posy asked Sharon and Jim to be Matt's godparents even though they were not practicing Christians.

Matt grew up in Atlanta with his brother, George, and his sister, Rosemary. George and Rosemary shared the same dad, but Matt had never known his own biological father. For most of their childhood, Posy was a single mom. This family of four would make annual summer trips up to Cape Cod to visit Posy's relatives. On the ride up, they always stopped in Washington, D.C., to see Sharon and Jim, who remained godparents and good friends.

When Matt was about eleven, the kids made their last trip up to Massachusetts together with their mom. While driving on the Cape with her father, Posy was severely injured in a car wreck. She slipped into a coma and eventually died.

"When the accident happened," Matt explains, "Sharon and Jim flew up immediately. They had the closest connection to my mom's life at that point. They came up . . . and that was just the beginning. It was the end of one life and the beginning of another. I remember being on the beach and the five of us were standing on different rocks kind of looking out at the ocean. They were really there for us."

The children returned to Atlanta, where George and Rosemary's biological father moved into Posy's house with the kids, and shortly thereafter adopted Matt. Sharon and Jim continued to maintain a strong connection in the children's lives.

"Sharon and Jim were very hands-on, touching and loving but not oppressive, letting us experience the grief," says Matt. "They were such excellent listeners. What makes them unique is that they do not put themselves first in any conversation. They would never give me the answer to a problem I was having. They would have me figure it out on my own."

As the children matured, the relationship flourished and Sharon and Jim became the auxiliary parents that godparents often are—adults who do not usurp the guardian's role, but who stand by and look out for the child's best interests while being a whole lot of fun.

"If I wanted to have a birthday party," Matt recalls, "they'd throw one for me. My eighteenth birthday wasn't just a party; it was more of a wine party. My godfather and I went out and selected bottles of wine. And I learned how to cook and be a host from my godmother. My godparents would throw these huge parties with fifty or sixty people. They'd serve homemade food . . . my godparents had both traveled to India and their cooking was influenced by it. It was almost like being with your best friends. You didn't feel pressured or judged.

"They were always open-minded and would never make me feel bad about whatever I was going through. I had this identity issue—I'm biracial and I look Hispanic. I don't look black and I don't look white. They supported me through my Malcolm X phase, my white phase, and through my fraternity phase in college. One of the most trying times for my godmother was when I joined a fraternity. She couldn't stand it. She's a feminist and thought it was the most idiotic thing, but she didn't tell me that until after I'd left the frat. She knew that's not who I was, but knew it was something I had to figure out for myself."

Godparents can become extended family members. They provide counsel, friendship, support, security, and good times.

Even through and after Sharon and Jim's divorce, the two proved to be an amazing support network for their godchildren. They put their own differences aside whenever they were around the kids; the divorce was never an issue.

"One thing that makes the relationship work is that I love

sharing my life with them," says Matt. "My godfather, who is Jewish, has been all over the world and has studied with shamans and is interested in stretching himself spiritually. He wants me to have the most amazing spiritual experiences and to live life to its fullest. And my godmother wants to see me fall head over heels in love. It's so amazing to be in this relationship. I feel lucky to have someone who is so interested in my life. My godparents [accept] me for who I am. I'm like a pirate's chest that is wide open and they can see everything that's good, bad, happy, and sad. They love me for all of those things. It's an unconditional love with no strings attached."

How Do Godparents Themselves Feel About the Role?

In May 2000, *U.S. Catholic* magazine published the results of its own godparenting survey of 164 readers and website visitors. The survey shed some light on the state of godparenting today and offered some noteworthy results. More than half of the respondents thought that godparents were "little more than ceremonial participants at a baptism." The survey found that only 3 percent believed that "godparents make a real effort to participate in the child's religious upbringing," which is what godparents pledge to do if they participate in a formal baptismal ceremony. Twenty-seven percent of responding godparents said they worry about not being able to do more for their godchildren, and only 35 percent contact their godchildren frequently throughout the year. And a "sizeable number" of godchildren said they didn't even know who their godparents were.

The magazine concluded that parents often fail to choose their child's godparents wisely, deciding instead to placate family members or friends who might not be committed to fulfilling the role. The survey respondents "overwhelmingly agree" that it is a big mistake to select family members out of a sense of obligation, without first considering the person's faith. Respondents also criticized parents who elect godparents based on visions of future financial contributions to the child, rather than what the godparents can offer spiritually.

In my own survey, I found that the majority of respondents had great experiences with their godparents and godchildren. But as a conscientious researcher, I must mention the possibility that those individuals with poor godparental relationships may have chosen not to respond out of guilt or indifference, so that my survey results may not be indicative of the current state of godparenting. However, I was able to glean from my respondents that although many of the godparental relationships had little to do with religion, the bond was a strong one maintained by mutual interest, respect, and love. The godparents in my survey considered themselves to be protectors, mediators, confidantes, friends, surrogate family members, neutral adult helpers, and supplementary parents.

If this is an indication of the path that godparenting will follow in the future, it is not an entirely crooked one. As we've seen, godparenting has taken on different meanings around the world at different points in history. And even if organized religion has come to play a minor part in the lives of some of godparenting's practitioners, godparents and godchildren can still cultivate a rich and mutually respectful relationship, one that enables them to grow spiritually.

Latino Godparents

Cultural differences certainly play a tremendous part in how the role of godparent is defined. For example, the Latino culture as a whole has woven godparents (known as *padrinos* or *compadres*) into just about every area of family life. And research over the years has shown that although the institution of godparenting comes with certain behaviors and expectations, each community creates and follows its own traditions with regard to a godparent's obligations and tenure. In many communities, padrinos remain involved in their god-children's lives, especially during sacramental events such as confirmation and marriage. A godmother often helps her goddaughter shop for her first communion dress, and later will help her select a dress or gown for her *quinceañera* (a young girl's official entrance into womanhood, marked by a celebration at age fifteen). Although it is not a sacramental ritual, a quinceañera is a major rite of passage for Latina girls, and the padri-nos often foot the bill for such elements as the venue, food, and floral arrangements.

Godparenting Among Puerto Ricans

Among Puerto Ricans, the role of godparent is taken very seriously. In the countryside of Puerto Rico, women who are close in age when they enter the god-parent/godchild relationship may seal it with a phrase: "Los siete sacramentos estan entre nosotros," meaning "The seven sacraments are between us." The phrase solidifies a sacred bond, one that frowns upon petty arguments and confirms the obligations the women have to each other. The women offer each other assistance—emotional, economic, or otherwise—during life's many challenges and hardships.

A dissertation called "Perceived Roles and Responsibilities of Puerto Rican Catholic Godparents Towards their Godchildren," written more than fifteen years ago by a Fordham University doctoral student, proved just how seriously the role of padrino was taken by Puerto Ricans. He made some insightful suggestions that pinpoint godparenting as a means of keeping broken families together. If reexamined today, these suggestions could promote some radical changes in how our social-service systems seek out placement resources for children whose biological parents can no longer care for them.

The researcher found, based on his study and a review of pertinent literature, that the natural support systems of Latino communities often take the place of formal private or governmental resources. His survey results indicated that the majority of Puerto Rican godparents view their role as a "serious commitment," entailing such significant obligations as providing a home for the godchild in the event of the death of either parent; providing advice, counsel, and emotional support; assisting with religious instruction; and offering financial assistance. When godparents were asked why they thought they'd been chosen for this role, some of the top responses were:

- I was perceived as someone who could maintain family values, norms, and traditions.
- I am respected by my godchild's parents.
- I was perceived by my godchild's parents as someone he or she could look up to.
- I could provide a home for my godchild if needed.
- I could provide economic support to my godchild if needed.
- I am seen as a good friend.

When asked to indicate a godparent's most important assignment, the response was unanimous: to provide a home for the child in the event of a parent's death.

The researcher recommended that the godparental relationship be used to keep children out of the foster-care system. In 1987, when the dissertation was written, minority children constituted a disproportionate number of the children living in poverty, and these children had a good chance of being placed in foster care. According to recent statistics from the

National Center for Children in Poverty, not much has changed: 30 percent of Latino children live in poverty today, outnumbered only by African-American children, 33 percent of whom live in poverty. But because the godparental relationship is bound by a spiritual contract or covenant—not a legally binding agreement—the willing godparents of a child would need to be presented to the social-service system as a feasible alternative to foster care if the biological parents could no longer care for their own children. The system would not automatically think of the godparents as potential foster parents.

The courts, when dealing with cases in which foster care is imminent, and social policy planners, when considering possible resources for families and children, would do well to recognize that the godparenting support system presents real options for children in need, even if the relationship within that support system is not legally binding. It might also behoove parents to assign legal guardianship to godparents, so that there will be legal documentation of the godparents' role in the parents' absence.

Mexican Godparenting and Compadrazgo

Researchers have examined the Mexican form of godparenting, too. A study of compadrazgo (the unique bond between a godparent and the parents who elected him or her) in Mexico found that the rural area of Tlaxcala recognizes thirty-one types of compadrazgo for which godparents or compadres are chosen, each with its own set of social, economic, and religious expectations and ceremonial requirements. Among the thirty-one types identified were baptism; confirmation; marriage; erection of a burial cross; graduation (including graduation from nursery school, grade school, and nursing school, among others); taking a mother to hear mass on the fortieth day after giving birth; ceremonial cleansing of a sick person; blessing of a new house; blessing of a new car or truck; first pair of earrings given to a baby girl; silver wedding anniversary; and presenting a child in church at the age of three. Researchers analyzed eighty years of local compadrazgo relationships and found that the average couple in Tlaxcala are asked to be godparents or compadres an average of ninety-two times. Parents ask adults to stand as godparents to their children. But a number of occasions are celebrated only by, and for, adults. In those cases, adults ask peers or elders to be their compadres. The institution resonates throughout the lives of the villagers, illuminating activities and events that are celebrated as rites of passage—events that go by unmarked in many other places in the world. It's difficult to find an area of Tlaxcalan life that has not been caressed by godparenting's gentle hand.

In Mexico's southeastern Yucatan Peninsula, the residents in the town of Ticul practice a more conservative kind of compadrazgo. They honor only four types of godparents: those appointed for baptism (these are considered the most important), confirmation, marriage, and *hèetzméek'*—a Mayan ritual that introduces a godchild to the tools of his or her adult life. In this Yucatec Mayan ritual, the godparent, carrying the godchild on his or her hip, circles a table on which these "tools" are placed. The implements are often displayed by gender. For example, a boy would be introduced to a machete and a girls to pottery or fabric. Like many compadrazgo practitioners, Ticuleños place more emphasis on the compadre union between adults than they do on the godparent/godchild relationship. And the godparent who is

In Tlaxcala, Mexico, thirty-one types of compadres and godparents are recognized. Among them are those chosen for the blessing of a saint's image and those chosen for the setting of a house foundation.

asked to sponsor a child at a celebration is given more respect than the other participants in the ritual.

Latino Godparenting in the United States

It comes as no surprise that the institution of godparenting remains strong in Latino communities in the United States. In the Latino communities in northern New Mexico, padrinos are assigned for three occasions: baptism, confirmation, and marriage. *Padrinos de bautismo* (baptism godparents) and *padrinos de confirmación* (confirmation godparents) are usually family members living in the same village. *Padrinos de casorio* (marriage godparents) are ordinarily a couple who are friends of their newlywed *ahijados* (godchildren), but don't always live nearby. The marriage godparents have the responsibility to see the new partners through any problems they may have adjusting to married life. The newlyweds and their padrinos also have a reciprocal economic responsibility to each other—the couples will build each other's houses and can each other's vegetables. In this region, the compadre relationship is so important that it supersedes all other titles when referring to that person. For instance, if someone's brother is also his or her compadre, the brother will be addressed and introduced as *compadre*, not *brother*.

In the late 1950s, researcher Margaret Clark did some investigating in the San Jose, California, barrio of Sal si Puedes and wrote a dissertation (called *Sickness and Health in Sal si Puedes: Mexican Americans in a California Community*) on cultural health issues there. Today, the neighborhood of Sal si Puedes (the name literally means "Get out if you can") still exists, and its former inhabitants' method of godparenting has been kept alive in the lives of many Mexican-Americans.

In Sal si Puedes and many other communities, parents would select four sets of padrinos for the four sacraments their children would complete: baptism, First Communion, confirmation, and marriage. After accepting the appointment, the padrinos must actually build two distinct relationships: they are padrinos to their godchildren and they are compadres with the child's parents.

The relationship between parent and compadre is ideally warm and friendly, but it shouldn't be playful. For example, if a potential compadre was prone to joking around with a child's parents, that person would probably not be chosen as a godparent. Compadres are considered to be as close as blood relatives; marriage and intimate relationships are strictly forbidden between compadres and parents, just as they are forbidden between godparent and godchild.

Godparents assigned for baptism are considered the most important. Because padrinos are chosen either from the pool of blood relatives or from the group of individuals who maintain close ties with the family, a godchild may have as many as ten godparents living in his or her own neighborhood. The godparents' religious function is to see that the child receives proper religious instruction and all the sacraments. (However, the community members agreed that although padrinos did offer support, they didn't often see to their godchildren's religious upbringing.) The godparents' secular obligation is to see that the child never lacks basic necessities, and to offer money or goods if the natural parents cannot supply them. Padrinos are also expected to use discipline with the child when necessary, with or without permission from the natural parents. And godchildren are more likely to heed the advice of their godparents than that of their own parents.

Because compadres are close—almost like siblings—they are called upon for help during troubled times. It's not uncommon for a woman to ask her husband and children to take care of themselves for a few days while she goes to the aid of a compadre who is ill or has just had a baby. Men will often offer money to a compadre who is not faring well financially. Both men and women will invite their compadres to come live with them if the compadre is lonely, has lost a spouse, or is out of work and has little money—even if that compadre in need has blood relatives who are able to lend a hand. And compadres are also asked for their input regarding important decisions.

It is even recommended that nurses take into consideration the compadrazgo relationships of their patients. If the nurses or family members are unable to get a patient to agree to treatments that health care providers think are necessary, the patient's compadre is often urged to intervene, and can prove to be instrumental in gaining the patient's cooperation.

Worldwide Variations

Godparenting around the world continues to surprise us with colorful distinctions. The institution is present in many levels of South American life. Among the Piro, a South American tribe, the woman who cuts the umbilical cord at a birth becomes the co-mother by performing this act, and relatives are called on for sponsorship during the initiation rites that usher a child into puberty. And, it was reported in the *Independent*, a London-based newspaper, that godparents in Sierra

Leone prosper at the wedding of their godchildren: godparents walk in front of the bride and groom while
members of the congregation stuff money into their
pockets. But one need not venture too far from home
to find godparenting at work.

Apache Godparents

Today, some Apache girls of the American West have
a *na'ii'ees*. A na'ii'ees (called the Sunrise Dance in
English) is a four-day puberty ceremony that inaugu-
rates a teenage girl into womanhood. A godmother—
or in some cases, godparents—represents the young
woman throughout the ceremony, which also serves to
reunite extended families and tribes, and reaffirms the
Apaches' link to their own spiritual roots.

The ceremony was illegal during the early part of
the twentieth century, when the government banned
Native American spiritual rituals. As a result, the Sunrise Dance nearly vanished. But today some families
continue to coordinate the celebration for their daughters, despite the time involved and the thousands of dollars required to arrange one.

Central among the participants in this elaborate and
well-planned ritual is the sponsoring godmother, a
woman who has been carefully chosen by the girl's fam-

ily and who will cultivate a special relationship with the girl throughout both their lives. To begin the relationship, the family members arrive at a potential godmother's home at daybreak and place an eagle feather on her foot as they ask her to accept this role. The woman accepts the role of godmother by picking up the eagle feather.

In an article published in *New Moon: the Magazine for Girls and Their Dreams*, a fourteen-year-old living on the White Mountain Apache Reservation in Arizona recounts her Sunrise Dance, paying special attention to her godparents:

". . . My mother and grandmother selected godparents for me. The godparents have to be spiritually strong, because they set an example for me to follow in life. . . . [My godmother] placed an eagle feather in my hair for strength and guidance. . . . I was massaged by my godmother so I could have a good life and become a strong woman like her. . . . While I danced, my godfather painted me with a special paint . . . the paint was a blessing for peace, prosperity and fertility."

Godparents in the Philippines

In the Philippines, children in Roman Catholic families are baptized when they are one or two weeks old and receive confirmation between the ages of five and eight years. The baptism and confirmation ceremonies have a social and religious significance. At each ceremony, a set of godparents—called *comadre* and *copadre* (literally, co-mother and co-father)—become regarded as the co-parents of the child and consequently are welcomed into the extended family. The godparents have the same obligations to the godchild as they do to their own children. If something were to happen to the child's natural parents, they would raise the child. Godchildren are expected to treat their godparents with the same respect owed to their natural parents. And the relationship between the parents and godparents has a specific and familiar name: compadrazgo.

In the Philippine culture, it is not uncommon to choose a host of godparents. One minister reported having conducted a baptism with twenty-eight godparents.

The Philippine compadrazgo tradition is shared with the Puerto Rican and Mexican cultures, within which godparents are expected to have a certain responsibility for raising their godchildren. Puerto Rican families in particular have been known to use it as a means of improving their children's lives when finances are shaky. It is not uncommon for parents to send one or more children to live with their godparents—for a few months or even for life—if the godparents' standard of living is better than the parents'. Various researchers have examined the institution of compadrazgo, and it seems that this practice has been modified to meet the needs of the families involved within each community. For example, in some areas it has been used as an economic aid for people in transition, such as new immigrants working through acculturation and assimilation, and as an emotional support network for parents when stress levels or deteriorating health become too difficult to manage.

It's easy to see how godparenting transcends culture—and often even religion—tracing indelible marks on the life maps of godchildren and their parents.

4

Choosing Godparents

We had to consider that the people we chose, whether friends or family, would always be there. [They had to be] the kind of people that have the same family values as we do through good times and bad. I don't think that one should make the decision just to avoid hurting someone's feelings. The decision must come from the heart, regardless of what others think. It's also important that these two people are able to provide spiritual growth from different points of view. The godfather we chose is a faithful Catholic, a true friend, and a wonderful father. The godmother does not have a defined religion, but she is spiritual in the way she lives her life—in her ways, with her own family—and has been a blessing to both of us by offering advice and guidance. And I feel that godparents and guardians are two entirely different things. The godparent's role is based on spiritual growth and guidance. The guardian is the person able to take care of your children.

—MONIQUE, Methodist

In recent years, churches have made efforts to help congregants—especially parents and godparents—recognize that baptism is a pivotal event in the religious life of both child and family. The church stresses the desirability of selecting godparents who can help the parents provide the cornerstone of faith and values for the child.

But even when it becomes clear how important your choices are, the decision isn't always easy. There are two things you may want to keep foremost in mind when you're making your choice: first, the requirements of your church (if you are following the traditional route to godparenting and baptism), and second, whom you believe can best fulfill the role of godparent as you have defined it. A godparent can be one of the most significant people in your child's life. You'll want to surround your child with people you love, respect, and trust: people who will support your children and who will make themselves available when beckoned.

That said, let's explore some of the challenges that may distract you from finding the right folks for the job.

Decisions, Decisions

This choice can be a delicate matter because it involves those nearest and dearest to you: family and friends. Besieged with possibilities, you may ask yourself: Do I return the honor of being named a godparent myself? Do I choose the friend who is closest to me right now, the friend I've known the longest, or the one who can best provide moral guidance? Do I ask the person who appears to be the ideal role model, or the unconventional, happy-go-lucky free spirit? Do I choose my brother/sister/cousin because he or she will be offended if I think my friend/colleague/neighbor is better suited to handle the responsibility?

And what if the person you thought would be perfect in this role considers his or her involvement to be a short-lived stint as a one-time, honorary participant at an afternoon ceremony? Can you really change his or her mind about the longevity of the godparenting relationship?

You may encounter other challenges if you're a partner in an interfaith marriage and attempting to follow the traditional route to godparenting. Perhaps you or your spouse practice a faith whose followers cannot stand as godparents in the church you have chosen for baptism. Even if those you've chosen don't practice a faith that honors godparents, you may feel that—for whatever reason—of all the people you know, they are the ones you trust the most to lend spiritual and moral guidance. If your choices do not meet the church's requirements, you might try to explain the reasoning

Unitarians don't consider godparents essential, but parents are welcome to appoint them if they wish.

behind your choices to the minister. There may be room for discussion. Perhaps they'd be willing to bend the rules; each church is different.

If the church is strict and unbending, you'll have to return to the drawing board. Maybe you'll have other ideal godparents in the wings whose backgrounds will meet what your church asks of you. But what if you don't? If no one else comes to mind, remember that you have the option to make personal and private choices. No one but you can sanction who can best provide spiritual and moral guidance for your child. No one but you can sanction who will have the most influence on your child's life.

If this is the situation you find yourself in, maybe a baby-naming ceremony would be a better fit. It would provide you with the flexibility you're seeking and give you the freedom to make the ceremony as grand or as low-key as you'd like.

Another obstacle may be the lack of appropriate family members to choose from, or a lack of close relationships from which to make a selection. Work schedules and busy lives don't always leave room for developing these kinds of relationships, especially if you, your partner, or your family tend to be private people. You may ask yourself, Who am I going to choose if I'm not that close to anyone?

What to Keep in Mind

If you're stumped by one or more of these concerns, remember that your child's welfare should come first. If religious conflict is a problem, decide how to iron out that wrinkle in a way that suits your beliefs and your hopes for your child. There is no easy formula; these are very personal choices and law does not govern them.

It might help to recognize that godparenting today isn't only about religion and religious things. It's also about faith and the presence that godparents have in your child's life. Your child needs to see these individuals in the context of their lives, with their values at work. For example, you may know a person who attends church regularly but has never supported family and friends in times of crisis, and in addition, is an unscrupulous businessperson. The church attendance looks good on paper, but what kind of value system can this person offer by example to your child?

The advice is the same for those of you who are having difficulty electing godparents because of the fear that you will offend a family member or friend: the welfare of your child comes first. Some families go through the trouble of naming multiple godparents so as not to discount anyone or hurt someone's feelings. It isn't necessary to go through this hassle unless you really want to appoint a community of godparents for your child. In the end, you may offend

Hinduism includes a baby-naming ceremony called the *namakarana*. It marks a baby's entrance into the faith, but it does not have a god-parent equivalent.

someone—but if the role of godparent is one that you consider crucial in the life of your child, that is something you and the person who may take offense will have to work through.

And perhaps you'll discover that there is no one in your life who is close enough or worthy enough to stand as godparent to your child. Don't feel bad. You needn't choose someone randomly just because "everyone else's kids have godparents," or because you've been made to feel it's the thing to do. So your child won't have godparents—it's not the end of the world. Certainly, your child will have many adults who will take an active interest in his or her life for many years to come. And these adults do not need to have a title in order to build a substantive and enduring relationship.

Give It Time

If you do have candidates and you're not sure whom to choose, you might entertain the thought of putting potential godparents "on probation." Babies are not always christened a few months after birth. You might want to try leaving a year between birth and christening, and using this as a probationary period for the individual you are considering. (You needn't tell the person he or she is on probation!) That extra time may just allow you to see who will take this job to heart. There's no guarantee that the person you ultimately choose will fulfill his or her obligations over the course of time, but waiting it out for a year or so may help you weed out some candidates you had reservations about.

One mother I spoke with, whom I'll call "Bonnie," confided that she made an awful choice for godmother. Bonnie had chosen a close friend to be her son's godmother. In retrospect, Bonnie realized that she'd never seen this woman (whom I'll call "Jackie") interact with children. Jackie, it turns out, didn't like holding the baby I'll call "Seth." Jackie was repulsed by the fact that Bonnie chose to breastfeed, and was disgusted when one day Bonnie, trying to juggle too many tasks, asked for help changing Seth's diaper. The new godmother even made an inappropriate comment about Seth's appearance—she thought he was odd-looking.

Bonnie was both heartbroken and angered by the godmother's behavior and regretted having chosen her. She hadn't selected Jackie as godmother based on her comfort level with basic infant care and feeding preferences, but she couldn't help but think that Jackie's negative and unsupportive behavior would spill over into Seth's adolescence and adulthood. She thought that if Jackie didn't warm up to Seth as an infant and focused on his imperfections as a baby, she would probably find fault with him as an adult.

Had Bonnie anticipated Jackie's behavior, she says, she never would have asked her to play this part in Seth's life. This is a situation where extra time between Seth's birth and his baptism could have revealed telling behavior. But Bonnie does have an option, since what is indicated on paper is not necessarily what goes into practice. If Bonnie and Jackie cannot successfully work out these issues, then Bonnie can always ask someone else to be an unofficial godparent. As a concerned parent she reserves that right.

Can You Change Godparents?

This leads us to the issue of altering baptismal certificates. Whether or not names can be changed on baptismal certificates varies by church and region. Some will say that names cannot be changed: that the choice of godparents, like the act of baptism, is irrevocable. Other sources will tell you that there must be a very serious reason for the godparents' names to be changed, such as their abandonment of the faith by becoming atheists or converting to another religion. In some cases, if there is a good reason for the role to shift to another person, the existing godparent might need to consent in writing to allow another godparent to step in and assume the role. The original godparent may be left on the register as a witness to the baptism, and the new godparent's name would be added, along with the date on which he or she took over godparenting duties.

> You might not be able to give a deadbeat godparent a pink slip, but you can ask a more responsible candidate to unofficially step in.

Regardless of what alterations are made to a baptismal certificate, an unsupportive and critical adult should not be allowed to have great influence on a child's life. Your child will have countless challenges to tackle throughout his or her life. Why thrust another hurdle in the path? Parents can always approach someone better suited and say, "I know you didn't stand at the baptism, but I would like you to take over as godparent."

What Qualities Should Godparents Have?

Here are some qualities to consider (in addition to what your church may require) when choosing godparents. They are not ranked in order of importance; they are simply some qualities you might want to take into account.

- Spirituality
- Genuine interest in your child
- Nonjudgmental acceptance
- Exercise of good ethics that coincide with your own
- Positive outlook on life/enjoyment of life
- Loyalty
- Trustworthiness

- Excellent listening skills
- Sense of humor
- Patience

Note that "financial stability," "material largess," and "has a great big house and big fat wallet" didn't make the cut. One of the most commonly held assumptions about these spiritual guides is that they will raise a godchild as their own if his or her parents could no longer do so. This is not how the church defines godparenting, and it is not the way the law approaches godparenting either. If something were to happen to you as a parent, neither the church nor the legal system would step in and supply a baptismal certificate as proof that the godparents listed could become the legal guardians of your child. As a parent, you should seek legal counsel to draw up a will indicating the legal guardians of your choice—whether or not they are your child's godparents.

5

Being a Godparent

My role (as an uncle and godfather) is to be a good role model to my nephew as an extension of his parents (my sister and brother-in-law). Also, in the event of their untimely death, I would become my nephew's guardian. My sister knows that I am very good with children and trusts that I would be a good guardian to my nephew.

—JOSEPH, Catholic

Godparenting may very well be the least understood role in Christianity, perhaps because of its varied religious and secular interpretations. You are not alone if you don't fully understand what is expected of you. Many a clergy member has grumbled that few parents have specific expectations about what the godparents they've chosen should do for their children. It's no wonder that so many potential and existing godparents are puzzled.

Many parents appoint godparents simply because they think they *have* to, in order to maintain appearances or to conform to tradition—almost like the pressure to have bridesmaids at a wedding. These parents give little forethought to what the role means to them and are sometimes disappointed with the way that the godparents participate or don't participate. And many a godparent has wrestled with the question of what his or her responsibilities should entail.

The Most Common Misconception

In the midst of writing this book, I caught an episode of a TV sitcom that dealt with a christening. The character slated to be godfather to his nephew had unintentionally gotten himself into a pickle, which ended up causing his nephew to arrive late to his own baptism. The baby's mom was livid. She told her brother-in-law on the spot, in front of the font and the minister, "That's it! You can't be the legal guardian!" The irate mother was going to ask another family member present to be the "legal guardian."

That's just not the way it works. If you are asked to be a godparent, it does not mean you automatically become the child's legal guardian when you make your pledge at the font. Godparents do not stand at the font with the officiant and sign legal documents after the water ritual. It just goes to show you that the role, and the process that gets you there, is quite misunderstood.

I talked about this misconception with a minister who is godmother to a number of children, and whose husband is godfather to several more. The couple discussed this one night and figured out that if all the parents of their godchildren considered them to be the legal guardians (and if the legal system did as well), and if something catastrophic were to happen that incapacitated all of the parents of these children, the couple would have twenty-five children living in their house!

What Is Expected of You?

If the parents who have chosen you are taking the traditional and formal route to godparenting, there may be some standards for you to follow. (There are parents who opt not to have a baptism, but will privately appoint godparents.) Some churches have specific requirements for godparent selection, but each church and each minister within each denomination is unique in their degree of leniency. Godparent suitability may be determined on a case-by-case basis.

Generally, the primary obligation of the godparent is to grasp the meaning of the sacrament of infant baptism, and to see that your godchild is raised in the faith—especially if his or her parents are no longer able to do so. Therefore, future godparents should try to attend any pre-baptismal instruction classes with the parents of the child to be baptized. If that's not possible, other arrangements may be made so that the godparents can be told what is expected of them. As a potential godparent, you may also be asked to provide a letter from your minister indicating that you are a practicing member of your church. Some churches, however, do not ask for written proof and only require that you have been baptized. Those churches will leave it up to the parents to choose appropriate godparents.

According to most denominations, godparents represent the extended spiritual community. But your lifelong role is dictated more by the family that selected you than by church doctrine.

Each denomination has varying requirements for godparent selection. For example, the Episcopalian tradition asks that a child being baptized have at least one godparent or sponsor present. That godparent must have been baptized, but need not be a member of the Episcopalian denomination. Catholics usually have two godparents, one man and one woman. One godparent must be Catholic; the second need not be Catholic but must have been baptized.

Godparents also turn out for the Baptist "dedication ceremony." Babies born into the Baptist tradition are not baptized until later in life (as with the Mennonites), usu-

If you were a godparent in France two hundred years ago, a great honor would have been bestowed on you: you would have been asked to name your godchildren.

ally during their teen years. Baptists hold that a congregant must be able to proclaim his belief that Jesus died for him or her and make a free-will decision to come into the church by being baptized. But a baby's birth does not go by unmarked within the church. A dedication ceremony is offered and godparents are present; their job is to teach the child about the Lord. Later, when the believer undergoes baptism, he or she is fully immersed in the baptismal pool as the congregation observes. Godparents do not have an official role in this denomination's baptismal ritual, but will often be in attendance.

Godparents aren't just chosen for babies. Those who are baptized later in life may have godparents, too. And they can choose who they want to have as godparents.

Ideally, if you are asked to be a godparent it means that the standards you uphold are valued, that your voice is recognized by the family of the baby to be baptized, and that they feel you possess a certain alchemy. The parents' choice speaks volumes about their perception of you, regardless of how a church feels about your suitability.

Your Vision of the Role

Before you agree to become a godparent, it would benefit you to talk with the child's parents to make sure you fully understand their vision of your future role. Perhaps you and the parents can map out a sort of blueprint. Each set of parents has different expectations as to what this role should entail, and each potential godparent has his or her own idea about the level of involvement that's required. Some assume the role only lasts as long as a baptism, while others envision it to be a lifelong mentoring position. Some godparents lament that they have made themselves spiritually, emotionally, and financially available over the years, but the natural parents didn't call upon them. Investing the time to talk to the parents before the baptism will help avoid miscommunications and start the relationship off on the right foot. Then later, you won't have to ask yourself if you are doing too much or too little.

Baby-naming ceremonies offer a break from tradition. They can be tailored to suit special needs, and parents may appoint as many godparents as they wish.

As a potential godparent, you should ask yourself these questions. Am I prepared to help and support the parents as they raise the child? Will I keep this child in my thoughts and prayers even if I am far away? Will I cherish this child and take an interest in the whole of his or her life? Will I have the patience to contribute my time during the difficult teen years, when children often need the most guidance? Will I be consistent about honoring the milestones in his or her life? How many times have I accepted this honor before, and will I be able to dedicate enough time to another godchild?

If you live a great distance from your loved ones, you may be concerned that geography will hinder your involvement with your godchild. But distance does not have to be a problem. In January 2001, an article appeared in London's *Daily Telegraph* that proved just how dedicated godparents can be when it comes to fulfilling their role from afar. It reported that a set of godparents located in Melbourne, Australia, were unable to attend the christening of their three-month-old niece and future godchild in Garveston, England. In lieu of their attendance, live pictures of the godparents were projected on a six-by-eight-foot screen in the church. By linking a computer to their television set, the couple was able to watch the ceremony and make their vows on behalf of the child from home. The godparents were thousands of miles away, but they found a way—via Web camera, modem, laptop, and television—to be present on this momentous occasion. Not everyone has these kinds of resources at their disposal, but with a little creativity, imagination, and planning, you can find ways to reach out to your godchildren from afar, in whatever fashion best suits your relationship and lifestyle.

A Lifelong Commitment

You may have asked yourself how long a godparent stays a godparent. About 99 percent of my survey respondents agreed that the tenure of a godparent is infinite, and religious figures agree. But what if a godparent, for whatever reason, decides he or she no longer wants the responsibility promised at the font?

You can't back out of godparenting just because you don't feel like doing it anymore. A godparent can't have his or her name stricken from a baptismal certificate or from a church registry because he or she is tired of the role (although, in some circumstances, a very serious matter can bring about a change). One person I spoke with likened it to taking a photograph on the day of the baptism—you can't change who is present in the photo or who made promises on that day. Those are the events that unfolded on that date and those were the people present; they cannot be erased.

Connecting with Your Godchild

Once you step into this role, there are so many ways in which you can nurture your godchild. You can start right away by helping the parents with their new addition. Are you a baby-sitter, an A-plus diaper-changer, or a handy baby-product assembler? The new (and sleep-deprived) parents will appreciate the extra hand, and when your godchild grows up you can share stories about the adventures you had trying to help Mom and Dad keep things under control.

When your godchild is older, one of the ideas you might consider instilling is the value of responsibility and sharing. The idea of service is an essential part of the church, and what better way to bring that idea home than for the two

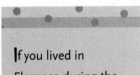

If you lived in Florence during the Renaissance, you might have been asked to be one of thirty godparents to a child.

of you to volunteer in some way? You might donate your time to a nursing home, soup kitchen, animal shelter, hospital, orphanage, or literacy program.

You can help godchildren pursue hobbies, studies, and dreams. Maybe your contact will be as simple as an ice cream sundae or a meaningful letter each month.

For the majority of people, godparenting is viewed as a lifelong role. Engage your potential godchild's parents in a lively discussion about their vision. Consider all their expectations seriously before accepting the position. Once you've agreed, you've opened the door to endless possibilities. You, your godchild, and his or her parents can spend a lifetime exploring them.

6

Fictional Godfathers, Fairy Godmothers, and Real Godparents in the Public Eye

———— ● ● ● ————

My role [as godmother to multiple children] is to love and nurture the children and, if necessary, help direct them to the proper guidance in the religion chosen by the parents. I take the role fairly seriously. It's an honor and it creates a bond with both the child and parents. I'm "honorary godparent" and guardian to my friend's child, who has a Jewish mother and a Christian father and is being raised Jewish. Celebrating daily milestones (first words, books, steps in life) and religious holidays are all a part of the package. When embraced, the role presents the chance to develop a special relationship with the child. It's a growing but constant connection between the two people that can lend the child a lifetime of support. I know godfathers who have "given away" goddaughters at weddings when the father has passed. Meaningful gestures can be made in so many ways . . . the role can extend the child's sense of belonging and family. My goddaughter nicknamed me her "fairy godmother." I can't describe how it feels each time she says it.

—ASHLEY, not a member of any organized religion

One of the most indelible cinematic characters of the twentieth century was the fictional organized-crime boss Vito Corleone, whose appellation is synonymous with the movie called *The Godfather*. The movie (directed by Francis Ford Coppola and based on the bestselling 1969 novel by Mario Puzo) has left two or three generations with a less-than-favorable image of what a godfather might be—thanks to, among many things, the film's closing scene. In that well-known finale, the procedures of a baptismal ritual are intercut with the scenes of a string of murders ordered by Michael Corleone against rival Mafia families. Michael Corleone is Vito's son—the successor to his empire—and the godfather standing at the font. The ceremony and the murders unfold in perfect harmony, and the word *godfather* takes on two meanings: Corleone is godfather to the infant being baptized, but he is also "The Godfather"—head of an organized crime family that has delivered death to many men.

The film sparked debate because of its violence, its negative portrayal of Italian-Americans, and the moral dilemma it presented. But despite the hullabaloo, the National Film Registry of the Library of Congress (which preserves America's film history) listed *The Godfather* on its honor roll of classics. The film is widely accepted as one of the most impressive works in the history of American cinema. Two sequels followed it, and the original was rereleased by Paramount Pictures twenty-five years after its debut.

The Godfather was budgeted at six million dollars, a figure that was returned many times over. When it initially hit theaters in March 1972, it became the first movie in motion-picture history to make one million dollars a day at the box office, and it has been reported that over the years, the trilogy has banked more than a billion dollars.

After all of this fanfare, a question still remains in the minds of many: how can a film that so distorts the image of an Italian-American family—a film so laden with violence, betrayal, and negative stereotypes—be so revered for decades? Film critics and scholars alike have sought to answer that question; many agree that we are drawn to the characters and their drama because they appear sincere in fundamental ways. One reviewer, Cynthia Rush, wrote the following about the movie for an article in *Theology and the Arts in Film*:

> Many scenes revolve around the elemental bond of food in the family. The kitchen is the place where family recipes are passed on from older to younger siblings and everyone gathers around the stove and the dinner table in familial camaraderie. To an outsider, the Corleones seem immersed in the sacredness of everyday life. They form a close family unit. Their daily routines center around going to church; sons and daughters marrying; children being born.

The trilogy may also have been so well received because of our insatiable fascination with gangsters, their families, and the glamorous and decadent lives they seem to lead. Whatever the reason, the films have helped many of us conjure up certain images when we hear the word *godfather*. All too often, we recall this all-powerful, much-feared character. But to an Italian or an Italian-American, the words *compare* and *padrino* mean *godfather in the spiritual sense*, and none of the terms has anything to do with the head of a major crime syndicate.

Fairy Tales and Fairy Godmothers

On a brighter note, our collective imagination has also been captured by the idea of the fantastic fairy god-mother—the magical apparition and eternal facilitator of justice who grants our every wish.

Cinderella is the heroine of one of the most famous, most universal, and longest-lasting folktales in history. One version of the story dates back to ninth-century China, where it first appeared as the "Yeh-Shen"—at least a thousand years before the earliest known Western version. One of the ancient Chinese manuscripts on which "Yeh-Shen" was based was written during the T'ang dynasty (A.D. 618–907); it places the events of the tale as occurring between 222 and 206 B.C. In this timeless story, Yeh-Shen is mistreated by her stepmother and stepsister but finds a savior in the powerful spirit of a fish, who serves as a kind of androgynous fairy godparent.

The story of Rhodopis and the rose-red slippers is one of the oldest versions of the Cinderella tale. In this story, a young girl is sent from Greece to Egypt to be a slave. Tormented by the Egyptian slave girls, she is ultimately saved by animals and a pair of dainty slippers that fit only her feet. This story is said to incorporate both fact and fiction; we know that a young Greek slave girl, Rhodopis, married the pharaoh Amasis (Dynasty XXVI, 569–525 B.C.) and became his queen. This version of her story was first recorded by the Roman historian Strabo in the first century B.C.

Korea has about six versions of the folktale that are all its own, and Europe has approximately five hundred more! North America had its version, too, with the Algonquin story of the "rough-face girl." Cinderella even made it to the opera house. Italian composer Antonio Rossini's 1817 opera, *La Cenerentola*, is based on a modified version of the story.

Almost every nation has a similar folktale, but the favorite would have to be the rendition by French writer

Charles Perrault in his *Contes de ma mère L'Oye*. Perrault amended the Grimm Brothers' gruesome retelling, cleansing it of its grisly details and sprucing it up with, among other things, the fairy godmother. (It is believed that Perrault may have confused *vair* [ermine] with *verre* [glass], thereby dressing Cinderella in her unusually fragile footwear.)

Perrault created the basis for the modern Cinderella, the fairy tale that inspired our love for the magical granter of wishes. It's no wonder that so many children refer to their godmothers as a "fairy godmother." Godmothers are revered, in all their forms, throughout the world.

Royal Godparents

Although high-profile engagements, weddings, and birth announcements take center stage in the news, baptisms and appointment of godparents also make quite a splash. Take Great Britain's royal family, for example.

It has long been the custom of England's royal family to appoint family members as godparents to royal infants; close friends may also be selected. Prince Harry, the youngest son of Prince Charles and the late Diana,

The late Princess Diana's younger brother, Charles, had royals as godparents, but Diana's four godparents were well-to-do commoners.

Princess of Wales, has six godparents: Prince Andrew, who later became Duke of York; Lady Sarah Armstrong-Jones (Princess Margaret's daughter); Mr. Gerald Ward (a friend of Prince Harry's father); Lady Vestey, second wife of millionaire Sam Vestey; the internationally renowned royal portrait painter Bryan Organ; and Mrs. William Bartholomew, a former housemate of Lady Diana. The selection of these individuals caused a bit of a stir among the aristocracy. Diana, Charles, and Prince Philip argued so long about Harry's baptism and godparent selection that his christening had to be postponed for a few weeks.

Prince William is one of seven godparents to Prince Konstantine Alexios of Greece. Like his younger brother, Prince William has six godparents: the former King Constantine of Greece, second cousin and friend of Prince Charles (Constantine also happens to be the grandfather of William's godson); the now-deceased Sir Laurens van der Post, a South African–born writer, explorer, and royal intimate; Lady Susan Hussey, one of Queen Elizabeth's ladies-in-waiting; Queen Elizabeth's cousin Princess Alexandra of Great Britain; Lord Romsey, grandson of Lord Mountbatten; and the Duchess of Westminster, once a close friend of Diana. Diana herself had nearly twenty godchildren, and Queen Elizabeth is godmother to about thirty. As a godmother, the Queen will try to make it to the christening of the new baby, and years later will make an effort to turn out at that godchild's wedding.

The Queen herself was christened in 1926 in the chapel at Buckingham Palace. She was dressed in the royal christening robe, which has been worn by all royal babies since Queen Victoria's first-born child—whom she named Victoria—in 1840. Victoria commissioned a lace maker from Honiton, a village in Devonshire, to sew the chris-tening robe. This heirloom, which is crafted of satin and cotton lace, is more than 160 years old and has faded to

Prince Charles and his eldest son Prince William have something in common as godfathers: they both stood at the font for the first time at age sixteen. Prince Charles was given eight godparents, and he is godfather to more than thirty.

a cream color. It is cleaned after each christening, wrapped in an airtight container, and returned to Buckingham Palace until the next christening takes place.

Following another tradition, many royals are baptized in the silver-gilt christening font known as the Lily font, another heirloom also crafted for Queen Victoria's first child. The Lily font is kept on display in the Jewel House at the Tower of London.

Godparents of Tinseltown

Robert Wagner, a veteran actor perhaps best known for his 1980s television detective series "Hart to Hart," takes his role of godfather seriously and feels it's a topic that's not discussed often enough. Here's what he shares about his relationship with his godson, stage actor Adam Storke:

> His father, Bill Storke, and I were friends. We met on the set of *Cat on a Hot Tin Roof.* Bill just called me one day and asked me to be Adam's godfather. I was there when he was born. I've watched him throughout his life, watched him go through school and take the direction and the desire to be involved in motion pictures and theater. We worked together

in the television movie *To Catch a King*. We traveled together, would go to New York together. I love him dearly. We had great fun together.

When asked how he would define godparents, Wagner says they're not supposed to be figures of authority in the child's life.

You don't have all the responsibility that the parents have. You become a total conduit between the mother, father, and child. Sometimes kids think that parents are criticizing them and not supporting them, that there's a lack of communication. The godparent is there to say, "Hey, your parents are doing the right thing." It's a backup system in many ways. You are able to encourage or discourage [your godchild] and support him and support what the parents are doing with regard to him.

Are any of your favorite stars godparents? Take a look at some of the godparenting relationships in show business and on the news:

- Lou Costello was godfather to Bud Abbott Jr.
- Don King is godfather to Pia Zadora's son.

Puerto Rican actress and singer Millie Corretjer was selected to be the official godmother of the Puerto Rican Olympic team at the 1996 Summer Games in Atlanta, Georgia.

- Actress and writer Kate Thompson is godmother to Liza Minnelli.
- Comedian Charlie Brill and his wife, Mitzi McCall, are godparents to Melissa Gilbert.
- Jacqueline Bisset is godmother to Angelina Jolie.
- Ol' Blue Eyes, Frank Sinatra, was godfather to singer Nikka Costa.
- Director Steven Spielberg is Drew Barrymore's godfather.
- Drew Barrymore is godmother to Frances Bean, the daughter of Courtney Love and Kurt Cobain.
- Grateful Dead bassist Phil Lesh is Courtney Love's godfather.
- Nicole Kidman is godmother to Australian actor Simon Baker's son Harry.
- Hippie guru Timothy Leary was godfather to Winona Ryder.

- Warren Beatty is godfather to Melanie Griffith's son Alexander.
- Singer Patti Austin's godparents are composer/producer/actor Quincy Jones and Dinah "Queen of the Blues" Washington.
- Karate champion and actor Robert Wall is godfather to Freddie Prinze Jr.
- "X-Files" creator Chris Carter is the godfather of actress Gillian Anderson's daughter, Piper.
- Phoebe Cates's godmother was film legend Joan Crawford.
- Singer (and ordained minister) Della Reese is godmother of Roma Downey's daughter, Reilly Marie.
- Shelley Winters is godmother to both Sally Kirkland and Laura Dern.
- Elizabeth Taylor and Macaulay Culkin are godparents to Michael Jackson's son, Prince Michael Joseph Jackson Jr.
- Princess Diana was godmother to the child of Rosa Monckton (president of Tiffany & Co. in the United Kingdom).
- Ex-Fonz Henry Winkler is godfather to Ron Howard's four children.

- CeCe Winans is godmother to Whitney Houston's daughter, Bobbi Kristina.
- Telly Savalas (star of "Kojak") was godfather to Jennifer Aniston.
- Sting and Trudie Styler are the godparents of Madonna and Guy Ritchie's son, Rocco.
- The famous French stage actress Sarah Bernhardt was godmother to French actor Jean Angelo.
- Kathie Lee Gifford is godmother to Bruce Jenner's daughter, Kendall.
- Film actress Jessica Tandy was godmother to cinematographer Michael Mileham.
- Carol Burnett is godmother to one of Julie Andrews's daughters, Emma Kate.
- American photojournalist Gordon Parks is godfather to Qubilah Shabazz, daughter of Malcolm X.
- Salsa queen Celia Cruz is godmother to actress and composer La India.
- Actress Mildred Dunnock is godmother to actress Maria Tucci.
- Actress Peri Gilpin is godmother to "Frasier" costar Jane Leeves's daughter, Isabella Kathryn Coben.

- Actress Jean Harlow was godmother to Millicent Siegel, daughter of the notorious mobster Benjamin "Bugsy" Siegel.
- Elizabeth Hurley is godmother to actress Patsy Kensit's son, Lennon.
- The Russian-born actress Alla Nazimova was godmother to former first lady Nancy Reagan.
- Liv Tyler, actress and daughter of Aerosmith's Steven Tyler, is godmother to Ella Rose, the daughter of Marlon Richards. Marlon is Rolling Stone Keith Richards's son.
- 1950s teen-heartthrob actor James Darren is godfather to Angela Jennifer Lambert, the granddaughter of Frank Sinatra.
- National Football Foundation Hall-of-Famer coach Forest Evashevski is actor Mark Harmon's godfather.
- The Dalai Lama was chosen to be godfather to the child of Richard Gere and Carey Lowell.
- Former Black Panther party member Geronimo Pratt is godfather to the late rap star Tupac Shakur.
- Latin music legend Tito Puente was godfather to drummer and actress Sheila E.

- Soap actor Michael Zaslow was godfather to actor Christian Slater.
- "Scream Queen" Jamie Lee Curtis's godfather is Lew Wasserman, a former CEO and chairman of MCA.
- Andy Warhol was godfather to actress and singer Bijou Phillips.
- Frank Sinatra was godfather to Linda Thorson's son, Trevor.
- Film legend Vivien Leigh was godmother to actress Juliet Mills.
- Late Beatle George Harrison was godfather to actor Dominic Taylor.
- John F. Kennedy was godfather to television producer Anthony Radziwill.

Blessed if by Sea

People aren't the only entities to undergo christenings and receive godparents. Ships are christened and appointed with godparents, too. Pre-Christian Vikings believed that human sacrifice was a necessary accompaniment to new beginnings, and so it was with a ship's first sail. The blood of a captive was used to crimson the ship's bow. The purpose of this gruesome ritual was to bring good fortune to the ship and all who sailed on her and to offer a gift to the gods of the sea. As Christianity spread, though, human sacrifice was forbidden and a silver bowl containing red wine replaced the blood of a captive at commencement celebrations. The wine was poured over the bow and the bowl was tossed into the sea. Today, a bottle of wine or champagne is smashed against the bow.

In some cultures, vessels are seen as newborn children. Their lives are believed to begin with the maiden voyage that leads to the place where they'll live: on the bright, blue sea. Like many newborn children, the ships are given godparents (sometimes called sponsors). The ship's rite of passage from dry land to water becomes a symbolic occasion that calls for a special celebration, known as a christening, a naming, or a blessing. The first recorded christening took place in 1418, when Britain's Henry V offered the Bishop of Bangor five pounds to christen the *Henri Graze a Dieu*, the largest warship of its time.

Like many rituals, the practice of blessing a ship has its taboos. One superstition is that the godmother who christens the vessel cannot be old. It was believed that the life span of the ship would match the remaining life span of the woman who blessed her, so the godmother had to be young. And even though in earlier times both a godmother and godfather were selected for a ship, it eventually was seen as bad luck for a man to perform the christening. It was also believed that the bottle of rose-colored bubbly should shatter with the first blow; if it didn't, it was considered a bad omen. It was also thought to be improper to send a ship out to sea for the first time without a blessing. Nowadays, a ship may sail on a number of cruises before it is blessed, and the old superstitions are not believed so much anymore. On occasion, a ship might be appointed with both a godmother and a godfather, and it's not such a big deal if the bottle of champagne doesn't break with the first smash. But one custom that has remained with many ship crews is to place pieces of the shattered wine bottle and a photo of the godmother in a showcase on the ship, as a reminder of the ceremony.

Sometimes vessels experience two or more christenings: not only is the vessel itself christened, children of naval officers are occasionally christened under—or in—a ship's bell. Ship bells have been used for timekeeping, warnings, and alarms, but their most auspicious use has to be the special place they occupy in a baptism. Performing the ritual on a ship is one of the navy's oldest and most sacred traditions. It dates back to the British Royal Navy of the seventeenth and eighteenth centuries, when chaplains began carrying out their duties on board navy vessels.

A ship is usually christened with a bottle of champagne, unless it's a German ship. German ships are often christened with a bottle of Moselle wine.

Babies born in foreign ports or at sea are christened underneath or inside the ship's inverted, water-filled bell, and thereby become citizens of that ship's home port. After the ceremony, the baby's name is inscribed inside the bell. While the ship is in service, the bell travels aboard it; after the ship's decommissioning, the bell may rest with the Department of Defense. Or there could be a potential heir to the ship's bell. The United States Navy may also choose to bequeath the bell to the first person whose name was engraved on the inside.

The role of ship godparent used to be reserved for heads of state, first ladies, relatives and wives of crew members, shipbuilders, shipowners, and dignitaries.

Eventually celebrities, sports figures, and other figures in the public eye started to christen vessels, too. Here's a glimpse of what's been happening in maritime godparenting:

- Opera queen Beverly Sills christened the *Song of America*.
- Actress/comedian Whoopi Goldberg christened the *Viking Serenade*.
- Olympic gold medalist Jackie Joyner-Kersee is godmother to the *Explorer of the Seas*.
- Tennis champion Chris Evert is godmother to the *Volendam*.
- Olympic ice-skating champion Katarina Witt is godmother to the *Voyager of the Seas*.
- Talk show host Rosie O'Donnell is godmother to the *Carnival Triumph*.
- Actress Audrey Hepburn christened the *Star Princess*.
- Actor Jimmy Stewart and his wife Gloria were godparents to the *Royal Viking Sun*.
- Queen Sonja of Norway is godmother to the *Majesty of the Seas*.
- Actress Lauren Bacall is godmother to the *Monarch of the Seas*.

- Former first lady Nancy Reagan christened the aircraft carrier *Ronald Reagan.*
- Singer Gloria Estefan is godmother to the *Nordic Empress.*
- Former NASA astronaut Tamara Jernigan is godmother to the *Carnival Pride.*
- Actors Ali McGraw and Ryan O'Neal christened the *Ocean Princess.*
- Princess Caroline of Monaco christened the *Sea Goddess II,* and her mother, the late Princess Grace, christened the *Cunard Princess.*
- The *Queen Elizabeth* was named after, and christened by, the Queen herself.
- Television newscaster Paula Zahn is godmother of the *Paradise.*
- Actress Olivia de Havilland christened the *Grand Princess.*
- Actress Jane Seymour christened the *Golden Princess.*
- The original cast of "The Love Boat" christened the *Dawn Princess.*
- Former first lady Rosalyn Carter is godmother to the *Sovereign of the Seas.*
- The Disney cartoon character Tinker Bell is godmother to Disney Cruise Lines' *The Wonder.*

- The late Princess Diana was godmother to the *Royal Princess*.
- Former British prime minister Margaret Thatcher christened the *Regal Princess*.
- Actress Angela Lansbury is godmother to the *Crystal Symphony*.

7

Godparents Share Their Stories

My role is to ensure that I stay in their lives always, and to be there whenever they call upon me. I would love to take them to church and teach them about God. If anything ever happens to their parents, I will be there to take on the role their parents trusted me to do. And you must remember to be their friend, and to try not to replace the parent, especially when it comes to rules.

—CHAUNETTE, Protestant

The best way to learn about the state of godparenting today is to hear about it from the families that have infused the role into their lives. This is what my survey respondents had to say about the way godparenting works—or doesn't—in their lives:

Godparents Define Their Role

I try to be a good aunt and guide my godchildren when approached for advice. I took the role pretty seriously. I guess [my role as godmother] should be over now that my godchildren have reached adulthood, but I don't think it ever really is.

—**Rachel, Catholic**

I asked if I could be godmother to my brother's firstborn. My goddaughter, Vanessa, is now five years old. My brother recently drew up legal documents to name me as her guardian if anything were to happen to him or his wife. I see Vanessa about once a month and I take my role very seriously, probably because my godparents didn't take on such a significant role. They lived in South America and I only saw them once every four years.

Recently, my godfather moved to the states and we've grown close.

I make sure I reward Vanessa for all of her achievements—dance recitals, arts and crafts projects. She gets excited when it's my birthday because it's the one time she feels she can give me something special. It seems that some people take on the role of godparent but do not follow up with what it means. I can respect that it means different things to different people, but those who don't take advantage of the special relationship it can create are really missing out!   **—Jennifer, Catholic**

I'm not sure why I was chosen to be a godfather, but I define my role as being a role model and a person my goddaughter can come to when she has a problem. I see my goddaughter at least once a week and I take the role very seriously. If something happened to her parents I would be there to take care of her.   **—Bill, Catholic**

I take the role of godparent very seriously. It's an honor to be a godparent. My uncle, who is my godfather, took me into his home when my parents

passed away and gave me love, guidance, and
friendship.   —**Theresa, Catholic**

[I consider my role to be] like a big sister or a
favorite aunt. I used to take my first godchild ice-
skating for her birthday and out for secret
hot-fudge sundaes that we wouldn't tell her
mother about. I think godparenting is a good
thing because it lets kids see you as an adult who
is also their friend. I want to make sure that both
of my godchildren know I am always just a phone
call away. Sometimes it is easier to talk to an
adult who is a friend rather than talking to your
parents. The role never ends. I think the "baby
stuff" (presents and little gifts each holiday) ends
when the kid is in college. But the friendly advice
and ear to listen will always be there.

—**Kelly, Catholic**

Why Were You Chosen?

My cousin and her husband said they wanted their
son to have me as a godmother because they know
how loving and generous I am. I've been a great
"aunt" to their three daughters, so they knew what

they were getting! As my godson gets older, I'll be there for whatever he needs—someone to talk to about school, his parents, his sisters, friends, faith, whatever. I take the role very seriously. It's my job to be like a second mother to this little boy. I can't tell you how much I love him. I love his sisters and my other "nieces" and "nephews," but there's something about knowing that he's mine—it's just awesome! There are really no words for it.

　　　　　　　　　　　　　　　　—Joanne, Catholic

I was chosen to be a godparent because one of my good friends was having a baby and was having a rough time with her child's father. I was there for her through her pregnancy and she asked me to be her birth partner, which was wonderful. I was there when my godson was born. I take the role very seriously. A godmother is supposed to be there to support the parents—or in my case to support the mother—and most importantly to take care of the child in case anything happens to the parents. That could mean a number of things, not just in the event of death or something tragic. It's kind of like marriage, I suppose—the role is over when you die.

I see my godson every other week or so. I feel like he knows me like a child knows his or her parents. He's a great little boy and when I pick him up he calms down and he seems to just know that I'm cool. I don't know what that's really all about, but it makes me feel good.   **—Shelley, raised Baptist**

I'm godparent to my nephew, Alex. He chose me [to be his godmother] when he was baptized. He was about six years old. I'd define my role as protector and friend. I'd feel responsible for raising him if his parents couldn't. I believe in a more secular godparenting role.

   —Maidel, raised Episcopalian, currently pantheistic

I don't know that I actually have a role [as godparent]. I believe that my being chosen was simply to conform to tradition. While I attend mass on a weekly basis, my family does not adhere to the strict teachings of the Catholic Church, and my godson's parents are of different religious backgrounds. My brother does not attend mass and my sister-in-law is a Baptist. They have not exposed my nephew to any particular religion.

—Anonymous

I think I was chosen to be a godmother because first, I am the mother's sister; second, I am a practicing Catholic; and third, I show a lot of love and concern for the baby. I'm not only an aunt; I'm the person responsible for instilling morality and faith in the baby and for providing guidance and advice for the baby and the parents. I haven't had the opportunity to do anything meaningful yet except to be present at the birth because the baby was just born. I plan on being there for the family no matter what.   **—Emma, Catholic**

My sister-in-law and her husband chose my husband and me to be godparents because we have the same values as they do and have the experience of a son the same age as theirs. As my godson grows, I would like him to know that I am there for him, not just as an aunt but also as a friend and mentor. If anything were to happen to his parents, we would take him into our home and raise him.

—Lori, United Church of Christ

My godchildren are the children of either family members or close friends. Basically, whenever I've been asked to be a godparent, the request was prefaced with something like, "I want my child to know that someone we trust will be there for him/her," or "The values I want my child to have are the values that you and I share." The role of godparent has lost its traditional sense. The godparent is no longer "keeper of the religious upbringing" of the child. We raise our children to think for themselves, to develop a set of values and live by them, and to educate their consciences in order to be able to do this maturely. In many ways, "godparent" is more titular than substantive. For example, I have one godchild who has yet to be baptized (she's twelve). And if, in fact, the godparent's role is to be one of parent should the parents be unable to care for the child, that godparent has to be designated legally as guardian. Oftentimes, the choice of godparent today is symbolic or duty-oriented. Like any role or relationship, godparenting will only be as effective as the effort and consistency that is put into it.

—**Mary Ann, Catholic**

I think my friend who chose me as godfather to her daughter did so because she likes my sense of wonder, thoughtfulness, and sacredness towards the universe. I believe she hopes that in some undefined way, this will benefit her daughter by providing a point of view, source of advice, or maybe just a friend.   —**Jake, nonpracticing Methodist**

How and Why Do You Choose?

In my family, the choice of godparents is very important. We've usually picked a very close friend or relative, such as a brother or cousin, to play the part. My oldest cousin is also my "godsister," which I think gives a tighter bond. Godparents are another set of role models alongside parents. I know that when I choose the godparents for my future children I will pick someone I would consider as another set of parents to them.

—**Ivette, Catholic**

When I chose a godparent for my daughter, it was because he is religious. He is a role model for her. Should something happen to my wife and me, he would be responsible for ensuring that our daughter got into a good home, though he is not expected to raise her. Her aunt would. Her godparent would take care of her until her aunt, who lives out of state, could get here. The most meaningful gift he could give my daughter would be to fight with the state for the right to choose where my daughter would go after our death and to ensure that she stayed out of [the state system], even for a day.   —Robert, Methodist

Since my husband is non-Catholic, I agreed to honor one of his godparent choices even though [the choice] may not necessarily meet my standards. The godparent that I chose had to be strong in Christian beliefs, live an ethical and moral life, and have a strong sense of family. Since these godparents are not a married couple, one godparent has been selected and indicated in a will as official guardian.

The most meaningful gift my godmother ever gave me was her constant communication and sincere interest in my life—spiritual or otherwise—even though we haven't lived near each other for over twenty-five years.

—Anonymous, Catholic

The funny thing is my mom didn't choose my godparents; they chose me. When I was a little girl, my mother and I used to go to this church in Harlem. One of the women took a liking to me and asked my mother if she and her husband could be my godparents. We went through the whole christening ceremony (although I was probably too old for that!). I don't remember much of it, but I do remember wearing a white dress.

—**Derryale, raised Pentecostal**

I chose my friend as my daughter's godmother because she was so supportive [of my adopting a child] from the very beginning, and because I'm positive that as different as we are, we'll be friends for life. Thanks to her, honoring special events is very important whereas I, a little less traditional, could simply let them slip by. She sent balloons and flowers when I first brought my daughter home and came over within days. She threw a shower, too, which was something I was decidedly not going to do. My friend has given a lot of thought to, and very much values, the role of godparent.

—**Laura, Protestant**

My parents had a traditional baptism for me in a
Lutheran church where my godparents stood with
them. [I saw my godparents] mostly on holidays as
a child, but I have not seen them in about fifteen
years. As their children got older, one became very
ill and required a lot of intensive care and all of
their attention. I'm sure it was difficult for them to
be godparents when their own child was so ill.
Today, my friend Ericka and I have running
campaigns. Hers is to be the maid of honor in my
wedding, and mine is to be the godmother to her
kids. I have no marriage plans and she and her
husband have no plans for children, but we
constantly make reference to our campaigns.
Ericka has other friends who also say they want to
be godmother, so we all jokingly try to discredit
each other and sell ourselves. After a recent visit,
Ericka's husband congratulated me on my weekend
campaign for godmother. He said it was the best of
all of Ericka's friends. I told him, "This is serious
business. They just don't want it bad enough!"

—Jennifer, raised Catholic and Lutheran

My godparents were chosen because my parents
thought that it was something they had to do—

although, oddly enough, I was not baptized. It turns out that appointing my godparents was one of the best things my parents ever did for me. For various and very personal reasons, I did not have a great relationship with my parents. (What I can say is that my parents were not ready to start a family at the time I was born.) Thank goodness for my godparents. They have to be the most loving and generous couple I've ever met. They made the effort to show up for every milestone (or at least they'd phone if they couldn't make the trip). I'm not sure how my life would have turned out if they hadn't treated me like their own daughter.

—**Anonymous, Catholic**

Memories

I did not have a godparent and was jealous that my brother had a godfather. I am pretty sure my parents' intention was to honor this good friend and didn't expect him to have any real responsibility for my brother. My brother never had much of a relationship with this person, but I was still jealous. When I was six, my family was close with a couple that was in their late forties.

The summer that I was eight, after many family dinners and long walks on the beach, I asked my mother if I could ask this close friend to be my godmother. I was so nervous. I thought she would consider it a big responsibility. The woman took the job and we remained close for years. It was comforting to have another adult to spend time with. She lived close to my school and I used to stop by sometimes unannounced and would spend afternoons with her. I talked to her about everything—my parents, my brother, boys. I think it's a great concept. I'm glad I had a friendship with an adult other than my parents to offer a different perspective.   —Anonymous, Jewish

I think it is an honor to be a godparent. Both times I was asked I was thrilled, because it makes you realize that the parents are looking at you as a good person and that the job or income you have does not matter. It is a matter of how you live your life and [being] the type of person that they want their child to emulate.

My goddaughter has been in Catholic schools since kindergarten. It is amazing to see how she has evolved from a naive primary-school being into a thinking young adult. She recently took a morality class in her high school and opened up to me about some of the things that were being taught and how she does not necessarily agree with some of the teachings of the church. For the most part, my Catholic-school experience was positive. But as I have gotten older I can relate to what she is going through. At some point you have to make your own decisions and live your life as a spiritual being, and not focus on what one priest says about a particular topic. I am proud that she has listened and learned about her faith, but has chosen to live her life as she wants.   **—Terry, Catholic**

My goddaughter died of cancer at the age of twenty-two, but I still talk to her in spirit. I spent a lot of time with her. We had a very close relationship. She was like a daughter, a baby sister, and in the end, a dear friend and my hero. I brought her to church to be baptized and watched her grow into a beautiful and brilliant young woman. She was the ringleader for her three brothers and their three cousins (my three sons). She was their advisor and defender. I delighted in hearing about her prom-dress hunt, read with pride her college application essay, laughed and clowned to keep her spirits up during her bone-marrow transplant. I held her hand and told her stories the day she died. I put the locket that I was saving for her wedding's "something old" gift in her coffin, as well as a piece of my heart. But as life would have it, I am also the godmother to her brother who has her laugh, so I can still hear her.

—**MaryEllen, Catholic**

When my youngest godchild graduated from kindergarten, he and I lived in different towns in Puerto Rico. His teacher asked him to bring a "padrino" to the graduation party. (In Puerto Rico, a *padrino* is not only a godfather. It also means a two-liter soda bottle. That is what his teacher was asking him for.) My godson raised his hand and asked to be excused from bringing his "padrino" to the graduation because at that time I lived in another town and worked during the day. His parents called to tell me the story. I was thrilled and very proud that the kid had thought of me, and that he offered excuses for me, thinking that I might be inconvenienced by the teacher's request.

Nothing would have stopped me from going to his graduation. He had won my heart forever. He was delighted to see me there.   —Carlos, **Catholic**

I have three godmothers, which is rare. When my older brother was six, he constantly whined for a sibling. One day, after church, my mother sat with three of her good friends and confessed that she'd been having spotting that the doctors could neither explain nor prevent. She was worried that she wouldn't be able to give my brother the little sibling he wanted. The three women held hands and encircled my mother and prayed with her. Two months later, my mother was pregnant with me.

—Cherise, **Pentecostal**

My goddaughter and I celebrated her first snowfall together. I asked her if she could hear it fall. I think it was an important moment . . . both of us very quiet, whispering to each other, having a moment together for something very simple. Milestones are what you make them . . . snow, fun, et cetera. The first ones are just as important as the ones that follow.   —Sam, **Lutheran**

One snowy winter night I was home in New York and I received a phone call from my godson. He was about twenty years old, and I hadn't seen him in more than ten years. He said he was in New York with a friend and wanted to drop in to see me that very night. We had a wonderful, spontaneous reunion. We caught up on a lifetime of memories until midnight when he had to leave. About ten years later, I saw him again when I visited his family in Florida. Each time we reunited was marked by mutually expressed feelings of a special bond, joy and unconditional love that was never cultivated, yet persists as a result of godparenting.

—Tania, **nonpracticing Catholic**

It Doesn't Always Work Out

I never see my godparents. One died, and I don't keep in touch with his wife, even though I know where she lives and she knows where I live. They weren't involved with me at all growing up, I think because they thought if they did get involved, I would become a financial burden to them. My father died when I was young and technically my godfather should have assumed a fatherly role, but he did not. They had many children of their own, so I think this contributed to his alienation.

—Anonymous

As a godmother, I complement my sister's and her husband's teaching and guidance of my niece. I see her several times a year.

I see my own godmother once every two years. My godfather is no longer a part of our family. At a family wedding, he broke down crying and apologized for being such a bad example to me. He had been unfaithful to his wife and then married the woman with whom he'd had the affair. I have not heard from him since.   **—Anonymous**

I regret not having chosen better godparents for my kids because I feel they don't participate enough in their lives. I understand they have children of their own and are busy living their lives, but it should be their responsibility to at least send their godson a birthday card, and [give him] an occasional call.   **—Anonymous**

8

Best Gifts from Godparents to Godchildren— and Vice Versa

My godmother passed away a few years ago at the age of eighty-two. She was happy and fun-loving. We used to be tennis partners and played many tournaments together. The most meaningful gift she gave me was her love of life, her optimism, and the fact that she never forgot my birthday! When she could no longer play tennis, I helped organize a tennis tournament in her honor to celebrate her eightieth birthday.

—MILDRED, Catholic

Most godparents would agree that the best gift you can give your godchild, by far, is your presence in his or her life. The time you invest will be the most meaningful thing you can offer your godchild.

Another great gift is listening. Not everyone is a good listener. Some adults feel they need to thrust their opinions on children (and on other adults, too), babbling incessantly until the person forced to endure it passes out in catatonic boredom. Please don't do that to your godchild. Think of all the opportunities children face for unsolicited advice: well-intentioned teachers, guidance counselors, and parents; doting aunts and uncles; busybody neighbors; and know-it-all friends. Your godchild, like everyone else in the world, will require a good listener from time to time as he or she tries to work through problems by talking about them out loud. Just button your lip and listen. Someday your godchild will thank you for your patient ear and contemplative silence.

As long as you're offering your presence, you are free to graduate to presents. What should you do about gifts for holidays, birthdays, and other occasions? Are you hoping for a stroke of inspiration? Take a look at what some of my survey respondents had to say about gifts given—and received.

I was so tempted to spoil, spoil, spoil my sister's children—one of whom I am godmother to—but instead, I put aside the money I would have spent on silly little things and when they graduated from high school, I wrote them each a "love" letter and enclosed a check for the amount of what I had saved over those seventeen or eighteen years, enough to get them started nicely in college. And I've received gifts. One Mother's Day, I received a telephone message from one of my godchildren, who recited a litany of gifts, experiences, episodes, events, and memories that she and I had shared over the years (she was about sixteen at the time). I felt the broad grin on my face and at the same time, the tears streaming down my cheeks. I hadn't yet recovered, and I played the next message, which was a continuation of the litany, with her adding that she had some "afterthoughts" that she wanted to share. She ended by thanking me for not only being her godmother, but for being motherly—voluntarily.

—**Mary Ann, Catholic**

I gave my godson a gold medallion of the Virgin Mary. I received a similar one from my godparents. My godson is only two; I loved it when he slept in my arms. That's a gift.

—**Belén, Catholic**

My godmother gave me the only new books that I ever received as a child. Years later, she gave me her gorgeous home in Ireland complete with housekeeper for two weeks when I went there on vacation with my husband, but the books are still the best. My godfather took me out to dance at a family wedding when I was a six-year-old flower girl. He bowed and made me feel terribly grown-up and talked to me like a real person—not a little kid. It's a gift to treat a child like a person. He gave me that gift and I try to give it to other children.

—**MaryEllen, Catholic**

Both of my godchildren were born deaf. I went to school to learn American Sign Language so that I could better communicate with them. I kept it a secret from my oldest godchild until I had developed enough fluency so as not to embarrass myself. I would give a million dollars for a photograph of the expression on her face when I first signed, "Hello, my name is Marcia."

—**Marcia, Episcopalian**

The best gift my godmother ever gave me was confidence. In high school I knew I wanted to pursue art as my life's work. For a lot of people, art is only something you busy yourself with as a hobby. That is certainly the view that most of my family and friends had. Everyone around me kind of pooh-poohed my inclination [toward the arts] and tried to encourage me to look into fields that are thought to be more "practical" and lucrative: accounting, law, research, technology. My godmother championed me and respected my decisions from the very beginning. Her words and actions gave me the confidence to follow my dreams regardless of what others thought of my decisions. She bought me art history books and drawing pads, took me to exhibitions and museums, and would invite me over for dinner so we could watch television if [a relevant art program] was airing. Today, I can proudly say that I've worked in several galleries and have sold some of my illustrations. I may even get the opportunity to illustrate a book! If it wasn't for my godmother, I might have given up the dream that became my reality.

—**Kay, no religion specified**

The most meaningful gift my godmother ever gave me was time. We were very close when I was growing up. She was only twenty years old when I was born, and I just thought the world of her. She spent an incredible amount of time with me—she always played with me and took me places. I was the flower girl in her first wedding and a "junior bridesmaid" in her second. She is one of the most intelligent women I know and also one of the funniest. As for a tangible gift, she brought me to my first concert ever as my confirmation gift. Air Supply. (C'mon, I was thirteen!)   —**Joy, Catholic**

I'm going to give my goddaughter a journal all about her. The first line of the first entry reads "Today you were born," and I've included the invitation to her first birthday party in there. I like to write things in it that are meaningful to me, which I think she would enjoy reading when she gets older. I write about things that happen when we are together, like the time someone fell asleep in the church at her christening; the first time she had ice cream; her first Thanksgiving, at which her dad said grace and said he was thankful for her. If her mom tells me a story that is especially funny, I will write about it by saying, "Your mom told me that . . ." Although I'm not sure when I'll present it to her, I do know that there will be more than one volume. There are memories in it I don't want to forget either, so I might make a copy of the journal for myself before I give it to her.

—**Debbie, Catholic**

My godson is nine and he seems to be leaning toward soccer as his favorite sport. I'm thinking of making him a scrapbook of soccer-oriented things: photos of favorite players, some magazine write-ups of good games, and so forth. Or maybe I'll place all of these things together and make a wall hanging. I'm not exactly artistically inclined, so I don't know how it'll look. Hopefully, he'll be so excited that he won't notice my shortcomings!

—Jim, Catholic

I think [the most meaningful gift my godmother ever gave me] is something she doesn't even know about. My godmother was a midwife. After witnessing the birth of my godson, I thought about becoming a midwife someday. That's a far cry from what I do now, but anything is possible. I know that I thought about her when I was considering midwifery. I know how much she enjoys it and I know that I would have someone to draw on, if and when I make that leap.   —Shelley, raised Baptist

The most meaningful material gift I ever gave my goddaughter was a gift of money to help her go to Italy and study Italian when she was a college student. She really wanted to go but didn't have enough money. It was a thrill to give her that gift of adventure. The most meaningful gift of another sort was to have a conversation one day that helped her to choose a career path. She was undecided as to a course of study for graduate school. She followed the path we discussed and it has led her to a very exciting career. That was the best gift I ever gave her.

> **—Zohra, eclectic religious mix of Christianity, Islam, and Eastern philosophy**

Respondents to the reader survey in *U.S. Catholic* magazine (mentioned in Chapter 3) served up some gift ideas, too. One godmother gave her godchildren a single piece of a nativity set each year on the child's baptismal anniversary. One godfather said that he is compiling a scrapbook of all the significant occasions in his goddaughter's life, with an emphasis on the religious ones. He plans to present the scrapbook to her on her wedding day.

Bear in mind that other family members will recall and celebrate a child's birthday and graduations. As a godparent, you have the opportunity to celebrate your godchild's baptismal or naming-ceremony anniversary. You can mark the occasion with something as simple as a call or a card. If you live close enough, you can make a date for a special lunch or dinner. Consider writing a letter, which seems to be a lost art in the age of E-mails and cell phones. A meaningful letter recounting special events or moments that took place over the last year will give children a sense of the importance and stability of your relationship.

Religious Gifts: Perpetuate Baptismal Symbols

If you've been diligent about keepsakes, you can use the baptismal symbols (the candle, the white cloth, the christening gown) or any symbols used in a naming ceremony as part of a gift later in life. Baptism is the beginning of an ongoing process in faith, and what better way to symbolize that process than to perpetuate the use of the mementos used to begin the process?

Baptism is also a ritual replete with symbolism; it is unfortunate that the symbols sometimes get lost after their use in the events of that day. Your godchild could use the baptismal candle during his or her wedding ceremony. Maybe it could be given to a woman as the "something old" gift brides receive in the tradition of wearing "something old, something new, something borrowed, something blue." The white cloth may have had the child's initials embroidered on it. Why not hold on to it and when your godchild has children, have the new baby's initials embroidered on it and give that as a gift for a special occasion—a baby-shower gift or at the birth of the baby? Having these symbols to pass on from generation to generation is a reminder of the continuation of a faith-based spirituality.

The following is a list of ideas for gifts—both religious and secular—that you can draw on to create or buy great gifts for your godchildren:

More Gift Ideas with a Religious Flair

- As a godparent-to-be, you could offer to help write up and send baptismal or baby-naming invitations or put together favors for the guests who will attend the gathering after the ceremony.
- If you are a frequent traveler, think about gifts while you're far from home. If your godchild likes religious gifts, look for rosary beads or crucifixes in different

countries you visit. Artisans craft the symbols in different mediums—stone, pewter, wood, ceramic. You can add them to an ongoing collection.

- Christmas ornaments are an easy thing to find while traveling, too. If it's appropriate, you can tell your godchild that each religious object or tchotchke has special significance. For example, "The star reminded me of how bright you are; the beads reminded me of your commitment to your faith; the crafts reminded me of your artistic ability. . . ."

- Offer a beautifully illustrated book of prayers.

- If your godchild wore shoes to his or her baptism, ask the parents if you may have them bronzed. Give the bronzed shoes to your godchild on his or her next sacramental event, or when your godchild's first baby is baptized.

- Offer your godchild a white-blooming azalea bush as his or her first-communion gift. Each spring its white flowers will be a bright reminder of that special day.

- Are you handy with a sewing machine or needle and thread? Volunteer to sew your godchild's baptism gown, and then offer to preserve it as a family heirloom for future baptisms—maybe the baptisms of your godchild's children.

Nonreligious Gifts

- Design a family tree and have it put on decorative paper so that it can be framed.

- When your godchild becomes an adult, or when he or she has children, offer to help compile a "family-health" tree. Trace all the significant health issues in the family lineage so that your godchild can accurately attend to body and mind.

- If you're a shutterbug, start a photo album of all the significant events and special moments in your godchild's life. Make it historic by starting with old pictures of the child's grandparents' and parents' wedding. Use a large photo album and leave about a third of it empty, so you (and the recipient) can continue to add to it long after you've given the gift. Make it a mix of black-and-white film and color, since black-and-white film gives a timeless appearance.

- Start a tradition with charm bracelets. Begin with one charm for the child's baptism or naming ceremony and add one for each special event, such as first communion, confirmation, graduations, entering the workforce, wedding, and so on.

- Offer a thick journal or a diary. Start writing in it on the day your godchild is born. Mark special events or milestones and write about how it felt to participate in those milestones. But don't use the whole journal! Your godchild can fill in the blank pages with thoughts and dreams as soon as he or she is old enough. It will be a collaborative effort that you both can read and share.

- Is your godchild approaching adulthood? Think about his intended career path and offer a key item that characterizes that path or would help her embark on it. Is he an artist? Buy a first set of professional paints, pastels, an easel, or a portfolio. For a teacher, offer a planner that will help with lesson plans. A seamstress? Maybe you can foot the bill for a sewing machine. You get the idea.

- Offer to open up a life-insurance policy in your godchild's name.

- Keep small milestones in mind to create meaningful gifts. For the first day of school, your godchild might appreciate a lunchbox. After-school hobbies present new opportunities for gift-giving: a jersey if your godchild has taken up hockey; tights if it's ballet; sheet music for a budding violinist. A sturdy backpack would be a practical gift for his or her entrance into high school. A Triple-A membership would work well once your godchild learns to drive. And what about milestones like a first plane trip? You could make up a "flight kit," including snacks and age-appropriate magazines and books. Notebooks, a thesaurus, and subject-appropriate books would be nice for the first day of college or trade school. And shouldn't everyone have a tool kit in his or her first apartment?

- Donate money to a charity in your godchild's name.
- Computer-savvy godparents can set up an age-appropriate Web page for godchildren who have ready access to a computer. It can be a collection of photos with accompanying captions or anything else meaningful to both of you.
- Each year that your godchild is young, try to find the time to make Christmas ornaments by hand. Hold on to the ornaments after he or she outgrows this tradition. Present the collection of ornaments whenever you feel the time is right: when your godchild moves into a first apartment or house, has children, and so on.
- Craft a quilt that illustrates milestones in your godchild's life, or includes symbols that represent important issues to your godchild (like peace, nature, wildlife, or children).

A Little of Each

- Create or order personalized birth plates. These dishes are engraved, stenciled, or marked in some other way with the baby's name; they could also be printed with the name's meaning and the baby's birthday or baptism date. Some birth plates are even dishwasher- and microwave-safe. You can also order a personalized silver spoon to go with the plate (make sure the spoon is lead-free).

- Check with your local baby store or surf the Web for companies that make personalized baby books; these books tell a story about the baby's first few days or weeks of life. They usually have color illustrations and places to insert photos. You can find Christian versions of this book if your role is more religious. Those books usually explain the role God plays in the child's life. Again, offer the book on a birthday, baptismal anniversary, or when the child begins a family of his or her own.

- Some companies will customize baby blankets. The blankets can be personalized with the baby's name and birth date or name and baptism date. If you are offering this gift for a baby-naming ceremony, you could have the blanket indicate the meaning of the baby's name.

- Novelty shops that specialize in baby items may offer many other items that can be personalized: blocks, piggy banks, keepsake boxes, rattles, gift baskets, pillows, candy bars, wall hangings, picture frames, photo albums, dolls, crucifixes, time capsules, baptismal candles, music boxes, rosary holders, statues, baptismal shells (the instrument used to pour the baptismal water), crib medals, commemorative plaques, remembrance cards, stuffed animals, keepsake baptismal certificates, Bibles, bracelets, bonnets, booties, and gowns.

Bibliography

Alexander, June Granatir. "Diversity Within Unity: Regionalism and Social Relationships Among Slovaks in Pre–World War I Pittsburgh." *Western Pennsylvania Historical Magazine* 70, no. 4 (October 1987): 317–38.

Armstrong, Marion. "Corleone Celebrazione." *The Christian Century* 89 (1972): 585–86.

Bauermeister, Paul. "Godmother! Godfather!" *Currents in Theology and Mission* 12 (Fall 1985): 33–36.

Bookbinder, Robert. *Classics of the Gangster Film*. Secaucus, NJ: Citadel Press, 1985.

Browne, Nick, ed., *Francis Ford Coppola's Godfather Trilogy*. Cambridge: Cambridge University Press, 2000.

Canessa, Andrew. "Contesting Hybridity: Evangelistas and Kataristas in Highland Bolivia." *Journal of Latin American Studies* 32, no. 1 (February 2000): 115.

Charney, Paul. "The Implications of Godparental Ties Between Indians and Spaniards in Colonial Lima." *The Americas* 47, no. 3 (January 1991): 295–314.

Clark, Margaret. *Health in the Mexican-American Culture: A Community Study*. Berkeley and Los Angeles: University of California Press, 1959.

Climo, Shirley. *The Egyptian Cinderella*. New York: Cromwell, 1989.

———. *The Korean Cinderella*. New York: HarperCollins, 1993.

Ericsson, Tom. "Godparents, Witnesses, and Social Class in Mid-Nineteenth Century Sweden." *History of the Family* 5, no. 3 (2000): 273–86.

Ethelbah, Normalynn. "Dancing into Womanhood." *New Moon: The Magazine for Girls and Their Dreams* 6, no. 3 (1999): 18.

Fagerlund, Solveig. "Women and Men as Godparents in an Early Modern Swedish Town." *History of the Family* 5, no. 3 (2000): 347–57.

Garrison, Peter C. *A Guide for Godparents: The Joys and Duties of the Spiritual Care of Your Godchild.* Lima, OH: C.S.S. Publishing Company, 1991.

"Godparents in Australian Internet Link." *The Daily Telegraph,* 30 January 2001, p. 13.

Haas, Louis. "Il Mio Buono Compare: Choosing Godparents and the Uses of Baptismal Kinship in Renaissance Florence." *Journal of Social History* 29 (Winter 1995): 341–56.

Kemp, Moira. *Cinderella.* London: Hamish Hamilton, 1931.

Kolatch, Alfred J. *The Jewish Book of Why.* Middle Village, NY: Jonathan David Publishers, 1995.

Kutsche, Paul. "Household and Family in Hispanic Northern New Mexico." *Journal of Comparative Family Studies* 14, no. 2 (Summer 1983) 153–64.

Louie, Ai-Ling. *Yeh-Shen: A Cinderella Story from China.* New York: Philomel Books, 1982.

Lynch, Joseph. *Godparents and Kinship in Early Medieval Europe.* Princeton, NJ: Princeton University Press, 1986.

———. *The Medieval Church: A Brief History*. New York: Longman Group, 1992.

Martin, Rafe. *The Rough-Face Girl*. New York: G. P. Putnam's Sons, 1992.

Martos, Joseph. *Doors to the Sacred: A Historical Introduction to Sacraments in the Catholic Church*. Liguori, MO: Triumph Books, 1991.

May, John R. *Image and Likeness: Religious Visions in American Film Classics*. New York: Paulist Press, 1992.

Mondloch, Helen. "Folkwisdom, a Global Enchantment: Cinderella's Dance through Time; History and Interpretations of the Fairy Tale." *World and I* 16, no. 2 (February 1, 2001): 180.

Nutini, Hugo G., and Douglas R. White. "Community Variations and Network Structure in the Social Functions of Compadrazgo in Rural Tlaxcala, Mexico." *Ethnology* 16, no. 4 (October 1977): 353–84.

Perrault, Charles. *Cinderella, or The Little Glass Slipper*. Translated by Marcia Brown. New York: Charles Scribner's Sons, 1954.

Rush, Cynthia. "The Baptism Scene and the Key to Hell in Francis Ford Coppola's *The Godfather*." *Theology and the Arts in Film* 10, no. 1 (1998): 40–43.

Sangoï, Jean-Claude. "Forename, Family, and Society in Southwest France (Eighteenth–Nineteenth Centuries)." *History of the Family* 4, no. 3 (1999): 239–59.

Schlumpf, Heidi. "What Good Are Godparents?" *U.S. Catholic* 65, no. 5 (May 1, 2000): 27.

Sheridan, Tom. *The Gift of Baptism: A Handbook for Parents.* Chicago: ACTA Publications, 1996.

———. *The Gift of Godparents: For Those Chosen with Love and Trust to Be Godparents.* Chicago: ACTA Publications, 1995.

Smith, Dwight, Jr. "Vito Corleone, Servant-King." *Christianity and Crisis* (July 24, 1972): 181–82.

Thompson, Richard. "Structural Statistics and Structural Mechanics: the Analysis of Compadrazgo." *Southwestern Journal of Anthropology* 27 (1971): 381–401.

Vidal, Carlos Manuel. "Perceived Roles and Responsibilities of Puerto Rican Catholic Godparents Towards their Godchildren." Ph.D. dissertation, Fordham University, 1987.

Wall, James M. "Confessing Without Repenting." *The Christian Century* 108 (1991): 35–36.

———. "Moral Outrage over *Godfather II.*" *The Christian Century* 92 (1975): 51–52.

Index

About the Author

Michelle DeLiso is a former public librarian, research editor, and reviewer at *Latina* magazine. Currently a researcher on the staff of *O, the Oprah Magazine*, she lives in central New Jersey with her three fellas: her husband, her son, and her pug.